£ 16.99

ANIMAL RIGHTS, HUMAN WRONGS

ANIMAL RIGHTS, HUMAN WRONGS

An Introduction to Moral Philosophy

TOM REGAN

ROWMAN & LITTLEFIELD PUBLISHERS, INC.
Lanham • Boulder • New York • Toronto • Oxford

ROWMAN & LITTLEFIELD PUBLISHERS, INC.

Published in the United States of America
by Rowman & Littlefield Publishers, Inc.
A wholly owned subsidiary of The Rowman & Littlefield Publishing Group, Inc.
4501 Forbes Boulevard, Suite 200, Lanham, Maryland 20706
www.rowmanlittlefield.com

PO Box 317
Oxford
OX2 9RU, UK

British Library Cataloguing in Publication Information Available

Library of Congress Cataloging-in-Publication Data
Regan, Tom.
    Animal rights, human wrongs: an introduction to moral philosophy /
Tom Regan.
        p. cm.
    Revision of the author's contribution to: The animal rights debate/
Carl Cohen and Tom Regan. Lanham: Rowman & Littlefield, c2001.
    Includes bibliographical references and index.
    ISBN 0-7425-3353-0 (alk. paper)—ISBN 0-7425-3354-9 (paper : alk. paper)
    1. Animal rights. 2. Animal rights—Moral and ethical aspects.
I. Title.
HV4708.R42   2003
179'.3—dc21   2003010538

Printed in the United States of America

♾ ™The paper used in this publication meets the minimum requirements of American National Standard for Information Sciences—Permanence of Paper for Printed Library Materials, ANSI/NISO Z39.48-1992.

From both of us,
to our children's children.

CONTENTS

ACKNOWLEDGMENTS

In 2001, Rowman & Littlefield published *The Animal Rights Debate*. In that book I argued the case in favor of animal rights; the philosopher Carl Cohen argued the case against. The present volume revises and enlarges my contribution to this earlier book. I want to thank Eve DeVaro, the philosopher editor at Rowman & Littlefield, for her help in seeing this book through to publication. My debt to Leslie Evans is large; the text reads far better than it would have because of her scrupulous attention. Finally, I would be remiss if I failed to thank James Sterba, co-editor of the series in which *The Animal Rights Debate* appeared.

Sidney Gendin and Dietrich von Haugwitz offered helpful criticisms of the book as it evolved. I thank them for what must have seemed a thankless job. As she usually does, Marion Bolz walked me through all manner of questions relating to formatting, for which I am so very grateful. As always, my debts to my wife, Nancy, are both broad and deep. It cannot be particularly enlivening to live with someone who spends most of his waking hours obsessively rewriting the same pages, over and over again, in the Quixotic quest to get every sentence, every word "just right." No day passes during which I do not count the many blessings Nancy unselfishly gifts to me, her patience not least among them.

PREFACE

Some people (and I include myself in this group) are passionate in their conviction that many nonhuman animals have rights; others are no less passionate in their conviction that they do not. The emotionally charged atmosphere surrounding partisans on both sides is reminiscent of other controversial moral issues—abortion and affirmative action, for example. For those people (the vast majority, as it happens) who do not have strong convictions concerning animal rights, one way or the other, it is hard to know what to think. I hope to provide some guidance in this regard.

Opponents of animal rights frequently describe proponents as irrational and emotional, antiscience and misanthropic. These characterizations may be true of a few, but they are not true of the vast majority of animal rights advocates. At least this is what my experience has taught me, after having been involved in animal rights advocacy for more than thirty years.

The argument I present in this book is one way to counter the stereotype of the irrational, misanthropic, more or less emotionally unbalanced animal rights advocate. The strategy is simple. We ask hard questions, explore the relevant possibilities, and look for the best answers. Then we see where these answers take us. When we follow this strategy, I believe logic leads us to a simple conclusion: many nonhuman animals have rights.

Some of the challenges we face arise in moral theory. Moral theorists ask many different kinds of questions, including two that are absolutely central: (1) What makes right acts right? (2) What makes wrong acts wrong? Different theories offer different answers. Despite these differences, every theory has something to say about who has moral standing (who counts morally). For example, some moral theories say that all and only human beings have moral standing. If true, the news is not good for nonhuman animals. If true, nonhuman animals themselves count for nothing morally. Other moral theories say that all and only sentient beings (beings capable of experiencing pleasure and pain) have moral standing. If true, and if some animals (cats and dogs, say) are sentient, the news for these animals is better. If true, these animals themselves count for something morally.

One thing we know. Both these ways of thinking cannot be true. It cannot be true that only human beings have moral standing, if cats and dogs have moral standing. And it cannot be true that cats and dogs have moral standing, if only human beings have moral standing. So, which of the two, if either, is true? When we give rational support for our answer to this question, we are doing moral philosophy. We will be doing a good deal of moral philosophy in the pages ahead.

Here are some of the hard questions we will be exploring:
Do all and only human beings have moral standing?
Do all and only sentient beings have moral standing?
What makes right acts right?
What makes wrong acts wrong?
What are moral rights?
Do all humans have moral rights?
Do any nonhuman animals have moral rights?

None of these questions has only one possible answer. This should not be surprising. Hard questions in physics or constitutional law, for example, do not have only one possible answer. Why would hard moral questions be any different? In addition to identifying competing answers to our questions, therefore, we will need to decide which ones have the best reasons, the best arguments on their side. The more fully we are able to do this, the richer our moral theory becomes. In this respect, our exploration of animal rights in particular serves as an introduction to moral philosophy in general.

Moral philosophy is not just theory; it is fraught with practical significance. This means that, in addition to asking questions of theory, we will also need to ask practical questions, including this one in particular:
What difference does it make whether or not animals have moral rights?

As we shall see, there is no more important question, judged from the animals' point of view. If animals do not have rights, then none of the ways humans exploit them (as a food source or for clothing, for example) is wrong in principle, and no wrong need be done if we continue to exploit them in these ways into the indefinite future. On the other hand, if animals do have rights, then all forms of our exploitation of them are wrong in principle and each should be stopped immediately. The differences really are this stark, really are this fundamental, if animals have rights or if they do not. Which is why, judged from the animals' point of view, there is no more important question than this one.

We should not minimize the importance of this question for us, either. If the rights of animals are violated when they are raised for food, trapped for their fur, or used as tools in research, then we will be duty-bound to change how we live, from the food we eat (or do not eat) to the clothes we wear (or do not wear). Nothing better illustrates, I think, how questions in moral theory spill over into how we live our daily lives than to ask about the rights of animals. True, issues like abortion and physician-assisted suicide have great practical significance; they force us to ask what we should do *if* we find ourselves having to make certain momentous decisions (to have an abortion or not to have an abortion, for example). By contrast, the issue of animal rights forces us to ask what we should do *when* we sit down to our next meal or *when* we go shopping for a new coat. Animal rights is an in-our-face kind of inquiry whose questions force us to make a moral inventory of our most common choices, our day-to-day way of living in the world.

As I said at the outset, I count myself among those who passionately believe in animal rights. But my passionate belief does not flow from blind emotion or a lack of respect for reason, let alone misanthropy. I believe in animal rights because I believe the moral theory in which their rights are affirmed is rationally a more satisfactory theory than are those theories in which their rights are denied. If true, then the heavy intellectual lifting moral theorizing requires ends with an even more daunting practical challenge: how can we live a life that respects the rights of other animals? I offer a partial answer in chapter 9. More complete responses will be found in *Empty Cages: Facing the Challenge of Animal Rights*, which I have written as a companion volume to this book; in the relevant references in the notes for each chapter; and in the resources available at www.tomregan-animalrights.com. While moral philosophy can serve as part of the begin-all of animal rights thinking, information from other sources is needed as we move on to the task of animal rights living.

1

FROM INDIFFERENCE TO ADVOCACY

I am an advocate of animal rights, active in the animal rights movement. This movement, as I understand it, is abolitionist in its aspirations. It seeks not to reform how animals are exploited, making what we do to them more humane, but to abolish their exploitation.* To end it, completely. More specifically, the movement's goals include:

- The total abolition of commercial animal agriculture
- The total abolition of the fur industry
- The total abolition of the use of animals in science

I am fully aware that some people view these abolitionist goals as radical, even extreme. Had it not been for certain events and the timely influence of various people in my past, the same would probably be true of me. I want to say something about my journey, not because it is so unusual (it isn't) but because it is relevant to questions I address in the final chapter.

I was born and raised in a working-class neighborhood of Pittsburgh, Pennsylvania. Education was a luxury the older people living there could not afford. By the time my parents were fourteen, they had quit school and, along with their brothers and sisters, were trying to help their families make ends meet by earning whatever money they could. Soon after my parents married, the nation plunged into the Depression. Work was scarce; wages were meager; scrimping and saving, they survived. This period of special hardship helped shape my parents' character. Fifty years after my father found steady work, my parents still lived as if the Depression were a fact of everyday life.

*Although I frequently follow prevailing usage of *animal* to refer to animals other than humans, I note that we humans are animals.

While shopping the bargains was their shared passion, food was one indulgence they allowed themselves. My father was proud to be our family's provider, and one tangible way he measured his success was by what he was able to put on our plates. For him—and the same was no less true for my mother—meat was more than something you ate; meat was a symbol of success. To be able to eat food that during the Depression poor people could not afford meant my parents were living the American dream. Meat became the centerpiece of much of what we ate: bacon or ham at breakfast on Sundays; salami, bologna, and other lunch-meat sandwiches most days for lunch; pot roast, pork chops, chicken, sometimes even a leg of lamb for the evening meal; and a robust, big-breasted turkey to celebrate Thanksgiving. In my case, questions regarding the ethics of diet not only were not answered, they were not asked. I dined eagerly at the trough of tradition. When the need arose for me to earn money to help offset the costs of going to college, I was not the least bit morally uncomfortable working in a butcher shop. Back then, I did not find butchering bloody, only bloody hard.

Fashion—being stylish, in a high-class sort of way—never was, is not now, and never will be on my screen. Not that I have been totally indifferent to my appearance. Over the years I have worn everything from pegged pants to bell-bottoms, Mr. B to button-down collars, penny loafers to low-cut tennis shoes, all in the name of being "in style." But haute couture was, is, and will remain oil to my water. Understandably, therefore, when the subject is fur, with few exceptions, it has had no purchase on my life.

What few exceptions there were saw me mainly as witness, not agent. Pittsburgh winters are cold. For some of the older women I knew, cold weather meant fur weather. Two of my aunts could hardly wait to don their fox stoles, and some of the women who attended my church were eager to make a fashion statement, flaunting their low-end furs for all the blue-collar parishioners to see, the unmistakable odor of moth balls lingering in their wake as they glided haughtily down the aisle. All this I observed as if at a distance, like a spectator at a ball game. Much later in my life, when I wanted to show my wife, Nancy, how much I loved her, I bought her a smart looking mink hat. She looked sensational, like Julie Christie in the Academy Award winning movie *Dr. Zhivago*. My only regret was that I lacked the money to buy her a full-length mink coat. Beautiful women *deserve* fur. That's why mink exist. At least this is what I thought at the time.

While in high school and also during my years in college, I found myself in biology classes where students were required to dissect animals. It never occurred to me to raise a moral objection; judging from their silence, it never occurred to any of the other students either. I remember fumbling through two sessions; in one, I was given a worm; in the other, a frog. The product of my inept labors proved I had no talent with the tools of the trade. I think I received a C − for my clumsy depredations. I know I did not like the smell of the specimens we were given or the sticky feel they left on my fingers. But I cared not a whit for the dead creatures whose bodies gave way to my crude invasions. During this time of my life, the worm and the frog might just as well have been globs of Silly Putty.

FIRST STEPS

In large measure, then, my beliefs about and attitudes toward animals were quite unremarkable throughout my youth. In fact, it was not until much later, after I had completed my graduate work in philosophy and joined the faculty at North Carolina State University, that I began to think about ethics and animals. The war in Vietnam was then being waged, and many people of my generation, not to mention many more of college age, actively opposed it. Nancy and I were no exceptions. Together with a handful of others, we organized North Carolinians against the War, a statewide grassroots group that sought to end American involvement.

It occurred to me at the time that war in particular and the topic of violence in general might be areas worthy of philosophical investigation. The writings of the great Indian pacifist Mahatma Gandhi were among the first resources I explored. What a fateful choice! For Gandhi challenged me to make sense of how I could oppose unnecessary violence, such as the war in Vietnam where *humans* were the victims, and support this same kind of violence— unnecessary violence—when the victims were *animals*. After all, there was no denying that parts of dead animals were chilling away in the Regans' freezer or that, most days, their cooked remains could be found on my plate. Eating animals, eating "meat" as I did, certainly supported their slaughter, a truly horrible, violent way to die, something I would later come to know firsthand when, despite having a strong aversion to doing so, I watched hogs, chickens, and cows meet their bloody end.

Moreover, from what I had learned about nutrition, I knew that my good health did not require animal flesh in my diet. So the logic was fairly obvious: the violent slaughter of animals for food was unnecessary. Was my fork, like napalm, a weapon of violence? Should I become a vegetarian, for ethical reasons? This was not an idea I wanted to embrace. Change, especially when it means altering the habits of a lifetime, is never a welcome prospect. So I did what any rational human being would do: I tried to avoid coming to terms with the question that was really troubling me. Instead, I threw myself into asking bigger, impersonal questions—about the justice of capitalism, the future of civilization, the threat of nuclear annihilation. But even as I tried to find a comfortable place for my gnawing sense of moral inconsistency, bedded down in the dark recesses of my unconscious, Gandhi's ghost would not go away. We never resolve conflicts of conscience by pretending they do not exist.

Gandhi had another lesson that festered like an untreated wound. People have no trouble living ethics in the third person. It's easy to declare that he, she, or it is doing something wrong and that he, she, or it should stop doing it. Academics have a special knack for this kind of ethical engagement in the world. We like to sit around and pontificate about why President X or Senator Y is doing terrible things. If we get really worked up, why we might even put some biting cartoons on our office door. By contrast, academics, like people generally, have trouble living ethics in the first person. The hardest thing in the world is to acknowledge that I am doing something wrong and that I should stop doing it.

This was borne out in my life. There I was, marching in the streets because the United States government was doing something wrong. There I was, demanding that the government stop waging an unjust war. And there I was, in the privacy of my home, still eagerly dining at the trough of tradition, preferring my steak thick, juicy, and rare. Gandhi turned this arrangement upside down. Ethics begins with the first person, in this case, me. The lesson? I needed to get my own life in moral order before I could get on with the work of changing the world.

As it happened, it was during this same time that Nancy and I had to deal with the death of a special friend. Early in our marriage, before our children were born, we shared our lives with a wonderful dog. For thirteen years, Gleco (as we called him) was our all but constant companion. Then, one day, he was dead. Gone forever. Such grief Nancy and I shared! So many tears! Emotionally, we were a mess, our sense of loss, so great.

From my reading of Gandhi I had learned how some people in India regard *eating cow* as unspeakably repulsive. I realized I felt the same way about cats and dogs: I could never *eat them*. How, then, could I justify eating cows and pigs, chickens and turkeys? Are moral right and wrong simply what the traditions of one's culture say they are? I knew I did not think that. Are they simply what our emotions say they are? I knew I did not think that, either. Besides, why should I feel differently about cows and pigs than I did about cats and dogs? If my emotions were really in focus, would I not feel sympathy and compassion for these animals, too? The more I thought about it, the more convinced I became that something had to give: *either* I had to change my beliefs and feelings about how companion animals should be treated, *or* I had to change my beliefs and feelings about the treatment of farmed animals. In time, unable to find a way around the dilemma—and, given the power of old habits and the gustatory temptations associated with lamb chops, fried chicken, and steak grilled on the barbee, I have to confess that I fairly desperately wanted to find one—I chose the latter alternative.

So it was a combination of the life and thought of Gandhi, on the one hand, and the life and death of a four-legged canine friend, on the other—a classic combination of the head and the heart—that first led me to ask ethical questions about the food I ate. The answers I reached some thirty years ago resulted in my decision to become an ovo-lacto vegetarian, a position I defended in my earliest professional publication in the area of animal ethics. Somehow, back then, I was able to convince myself that while it was wrong to eat animals, it was all right to eat eggs and dairy products as part of my everyday diet.

A LARGER CONSISTENCY

That first step toward including nonhuman animals in my moral universe was soon followed by others. You might say Leo Tolstoy predicted as much. In his classic essay "The First Step" Tolstoy writes that one way people can attempt to grow in the direction of a more peaceful, less violent way of life is to stop eating animals. Tolstoy does not mean that giving up meat necessarily makes one a better person; he does not even mean that meat eaters necessarily are bad people; what he means is that the decision to become a vegetarian, when rooted in the quest for a less violent way of being in the world, is a first step some people can take.

Once having taken this first step, Tolstoy believes that those who begin their journey (and Nancy was alongside or ahead of me throughout the years of change) are all but certain to attempt to move in the direction of a larger consistency. The more I studied the animal ingredients in popular brands of household cleaners and cosmetics, for example, and the more I learned about the painful tests manufacturers routinely perform on animals, the more committed I became to using cruelty-free products: detergents and cleaners, shampoos and deodorants, soaps and toothpastes that do not contain anything of animal origin and that have not been tested on animals. I also realized that fur was not compatible with the kind of life I wanted to live. A mink hat might be warm; it might be stylish; and some women might look stunningly beautiful wearing one. All this I knew. But that did not make the violent death of fur-bearing animals any less unnecessary. Such is the human mind's capacity for self-deception, however, that even as purchasing fur had become unthinkable, I continued to find no inconsistency in wearing leather belts, gloves, and shoes or in buying wool pants, sweaters, and jackets. I was in my bell-bottom, penny-loafer phase.

As for the use of animals in science, that was the last question I approached, and my first thoughts stopped well short of the abolitionist ones I hold today. Even while I called for "a vast reduction in research involving animals," I left open the possibility that some of this research could be justified. What sort of research would this be? Where did I draw the line? Suffice it to say that during this period of my life, hard as it is to understand today, I defended major auto manufacturers, like General Motors, when they killed baboons in crash tests designed to make seat belts safer.

The preceding few pages should go some way toward suggesting just how far the "radical" and "extreme" abolitionist views I hold today are from those I accepted while I was growing up and how much they differ, too, from the answers I gave when I first began asking ethical questions about how we humans treat other animals. I was not born an animal rights abolitionist, but along with Nancy and millions of others, I have become one, not all at once, but gradually. Animal rights advocacy was the unanticipated destination toward which a line of reasoning and transforming experiences would lead us. A dog's death was one of those experiences; watching animals bleed to death at their slaughter was another; still others, in which we learned more about the terrible things human beings do to animal beings, were to follow.

LOOKING AHEAD

How *do* we treat other animals? What actually happens to them on the farm, in the wild, and at the research lab? While it is not possible to give anything like complete answers to these questions, it is necessary to provide some of the relevant facts. When the topic is animal rights, we are not dealing with imaginary beings like Winnie the Pooh or E. T.; we are dealing with flesh-and-blood creatures who breathe the same air and who live and die on the same planet, as we do. Granted, facts about their treatment do not prove that animals have rights. What these facts can suggest is the magnitude of the evil done to them, if they do. Chapter 2 makes good on the need to provide some of the relevant facts by highlighting aspects of how animals are treated in the food industry, the fur industry, and the research industry.

Beginning with chapter 3, the discussion takes a philosophical turn. In the not too distant past, the topic of animal rights was laughed out of the court of serious philosophical discussion. In the latter part of the eighteenth century, for example, the distinguished English philosopher Thomas Taylor published *A Vindication of the Rights of Brutes*, a comic proposal meant to satirize the idea that women could have rights. More than a hundred years later, Father Joseph Rickaby spoke for the dominant philosophical orthodoxy of the time when he characterized the moral standing of animals as "[being] of the order of sticks and stones." Times have changed. More has been written on the rights of animals in the past thirty years than was written on this topic in the previous three thousand. Today, asking whether animals have rights is recognized as a serious, challenging philosophical question, one that cannot be given the systematic attention it deserves in the absence of at least a working knowledge of what moral philosophers mean when they speak of individual rights. Chapter 3 attempts to provide the necessary clarification. No arguments are offered there, either for human or animal rights. These arguments will be found in chapters 6 and 7, respectively. My far more limited objective in chapter 3 is to explain what rights are and why having them (if anyone does) is so important.

While there are exceptions to the rule, moral philosophers as a group aspire to offer general accounts of moral right and wrong; fundamentally, what they want to know is not whether a particular action, policy, or law is right or wrong but what makes any action, policy, or law right or wrong. Some influential ways to think about moral right and wrong at this level deny rights across the board: animals do not have rights, they say, but neither do humans. Other positions, while they deny rights to animals, affirm them in the case of humans. Representative examples of these moral outlooks are examined in chapters 4 and 5, which also provide the setting for examining the existence and complexity of animal minds. Each of the moral theories considered has something to recommend it. No moral theory—none with which I am familiar, in any event—fails to say something true, something important; so even while I explain where and why I think each of these theories has various weaknesses, I also think each has strengths worth preserving.

Having explained some of the deficiencies of the moral theories discussed in these two chapters, I then explain in chapter 6 how some of these weaknesses can be overcome if human rights are recognized. The conclusions reached in this chapter are essential to how I think about morality, not only because of the role they play in my cumulative argument for animal rights but also because of the importance human rights occupy in my life and thought. As I will explain, my commitment to human rights is, if anything, even more central to my moral outlook than is my commitment to animal rights. Those looking for misanthropy among animal rights advocates will not find it here.

After making my case for human rights, I turn (in chapter 7) to the topic of animal rights and explain how recognition of their rights emerges from, and is dependent upon, the conclusions reached in the preceding three chapters, including in particular my argument for human rights. Chapter 8 explores a variety of general, religious, and philosophical objections to animal rights. This is followed by a final chapter that draws together themes and topics considered along the way, including the "radical," "extreme" nature of my abolitionist beliefs. Sometimes, I argue, radical, extreme ideas are where the moral truth lies, the abolitionist implications of animal rights being a case in point. Also considered are vexing questions about the relationship between moral philosophy and human motivation. First, though, we turn to some facts about how animals are treated, not in exceptional circumstances but as a matter of everyday, ordinary practice.

2

ANIMAL EXPLOITATION

We humans kill billions of animals every year, just in America. Frequently what we do causes them intense physical pain; often they are made to live in deplorable conditions; in many, possibly the majority, of cases, they go to their deaths without having had the opportunity to satisfy many of their most basic desires. Readers interested in gaining a more complete grasp of animal exploitation, both in the United States and globally, will find what they are looking for by consulting the resources mentioned at the end of the preface. What follows is at most a thumbnail sketch of a few of the ways human beings treat animal beings in three institutional contexts: agriculture, fashion, and science.

ANIMALS AS FOOD

Veal, especially so-called pink or milk-fed veal, is the centerpiece in what some people regard as the finest dishes, prepared by the finest chefs, and served in the finest restaurants, especially French and Italian restaurants. Famous for its tenderness, milk-fed veal can be cut with a fork. No gristle. No muscle. Just soft, unresisting flesh that melts in your mouth. When it comes to good eating, some people find it hard to imagine how it can get any better than this.

The situation is different for the calves who end up as veal. Veal calves (or "special fed veal," as they are also known) are surplus calves, most of them bull calves born to Holstein dairy herds. While the majority of the surplus calves, both male and female, are raised and sold as beef in America, approximately eight hundred thousand annually enter and exit a market of their own. That market is the special-fed or milk-fed veal industry.

Calves who enter this industry are taken from their mothers hours or days (less than seven days is the industry's recommendation) after they are born, then sold at auction or delivered to contract vealers. Throughout most of history, demand for pink veal outstripped supply. Calves were slaughtered when they were very young, before they consumed too much iron-rich foods, like their mother's milk or grass, which would turn their flesh from pink to red and reduce consumer demand.

Understandably, these animals were not large, weighing in at only about ninety pounds. Because they were so small, the supply of their tender, pink flesh was limited and the price per pound high. Predictably, premium veal found its way onto the dinner plates only of the wealthy. In time things changed, first in Europe in the 1950s, then in the 1960s in the United States. A new production system was introduced that enabled veal calves to live four or five months, during which time they more than tripled their birth weight, without the calves' flesh losing its desired pale color and tenderness. With the advent of larger calves, the industry offered milk-fed veal to an expanded market by selling it at a more affordable price.

For the system to work, milk-fed veal calves are permanently confined in individual stalls. Recommended stall dimensions in the United States are 24 inches wide by 65 inches long. Veal production systems can range from 50 to more than 3,000 stalls, with 200 the average. Of the approximately 1,400 systems in the United States, most are found in Indiana, Michigan, New York, Pennsylvania, and Wisconsin. Approximately 450 are located in Pennsylvania alone.

Because calves lick their surroundings, because metal box stalls contain iron, and because extra iron can help turn their flesh red, the stalls are made of wood. *The Stall Street Journal*, a now defunct veal industry newsletter, explains: "Color of veal is one of the primary factors involved in obtaining 'top dollar' returns from the fancy veal markets. . . . 'Light color' veal is a premium item much in demand at better clubs, hotels and restaurants. 'Light color' or pink veal is partly associated with the amount of iron in the muscle of calves."

Of course, if iron is totally eliminated from their diet, the calves' lives could be placed in jeopardy, as would the farmers' financial interests. So *some* iron is included in the total liquid diet (a combination of nonfat powdered milk, vitamins, minerals, sugar, antibiotics, and growth-enhancing drugs) the calves are fed twice a day, throughout the duration of their short lives. This, not their mother's milk, is the dietary history of so-called milk-fed veal.

To withhold real milk and other plentiful sources of iron from veal calves makes perfectly good sense to veal producers. In the words of *The Stall Street*

Journal, "the dual aims of veal production are firstly, to produce a calf of the greatest weight in the shortest possible time and, secondly, to keep its meat as light colored as possible to fulfill the consumer's requirement." For calves, this means being raised in a chronically iron-deficient (that is to say, a chronically anemic) condition.

When the calves are small and able to turn around in their stalls, a metal or plastic tether prevents them from doing so. Later, when they are three or four hundred pounds and too large to turn around in their narrow enclosures, the tether may be removed. Whether tethered or not, the animals are all but immobilized. Calves are notorious for their friskiness. We all have seen these boisterous youngsters gamboling across spacious pastures, their tender muscles firming up to support their increasing weight. Not so the calves raised in veal crates. The conditions of their confinement insure that their muscles will remain limp so their flesh retains the degree of tenderness that, in the words of the *Journal*, "fulfill(s) the consumers' requirement."

The stalls in which individual calves are confined have slatted floors made either of wood or metal covered with plastic. In theory, the openings between the slats prevent urine and excrement from collecting. The theory does not work well in practice. When the animals lie down, they lie in their own waste. When they stand, their footing is unsure on the slippery slats. Unable to turn around, the calves cannot clean themselves. Unable to move without the prospect of slipping, they learn to stand in one place for long periods of time, a passive adjustment to their surroundings that takes its toll on their anatomy, especially their knees, which often are discernibly swollen and painful.

Independent scientific observers have confirmed what people of plain common sense already know. Veal calves suffer both physically and psychologically. Physically, they suffer because the majority of these animals endure the pain and discomfort of swollen joints, digestive disorders, and chronic diarrhea. Psychologically, they suffer because their lives of solitary confinement are characterized by abject deprivation. Throughout their lives they are denied the opportunity to suckle and graze; denied the opportunity to stretch their legs; denied the fresh air and sunlight they naturally enjoy.

In a word, calves raised in veal crates are denied virtually everything that answers to their nature. That they display behavioral patterns (for example, repetitive movements and tongue rolling) associated with psychological maladjustment should surprise no one. These animals are not well, not in body, not in mind. When the day arrives for them to go to their foreordained slaughter, not as the frolicsome creatures they might have been but as the stunted "fancy" meat machines their producers and consumers have made them, death offers these forlorn animals a better bargain than the lives they have known.

Factory Farming

Compared with the other animals raised for human consumption, the total number of milk-fed veal calves who end up on America's dinner plates is small—some eight hundred thousand of the approximately *ten billion* farmed animals slaughtered annually, more than twenty-seven million every day, in excess of a million every hour, just in the United States. But while their number is small, the lifeway of "milk-fed" veal calves is a microcosm of the larger reality of commercial animal agriculture as it is practiced today.

The myth of Old McDonald's Farm dies hard. Whatever the reasons, and in the face of years of exposure by animal rights advocates showing the opposite, many people persist in believing that farmed animals live in bucolic conditions. The truth is another matter. The vast majority of animals who enter and exit through the doors of today's commercial animal industry live lives not very different from those of veal calves. Intensive rearing systems ("factory farms") are the rule, not the exception. Hogs, chickens, turkeys, and other animals raised for human consumption, not just veal calves, have become so many biological machines.

The reasons behind the ascendancy of factory farming are not hard to find. The profit motive, aided by government subsidies and price supports, drives the industry. Animal agriculture is a business, after all, whose object is to maximize financial return while minimizing financial investment. The key to financial success is a variation on the main theme found in veal production.

Factory farming requires that animals be taken off the land and raised indoors. This is important. Indoor farming enables a comparatively few people to raise hundreds, sometimes (as is true in the case of laying hens and broiler chickens) hundreds of thousands of animals, something that would be impossible if the animals were free to roam.

Next, farmers must do whatever is necessary to bring the animals to market in the shortest possible time. Measures that might be taken include limiting the animals' mobility, manipulating their appetite so that they eat more than they would in natural conditions, and stimulating their weight gain by including growth-enhancing hormones in their feed. In the words of *The Stall Street Journal*, it is essential "to produce a calf [or a chicken or a hog, for example] of the greatest weight in the shortest possible time." Those farmers who fail the test fail in the marketplace of commercial animal agriculture. And many do. Unable to compete with their large corporate neighbors, powerless against the economies of scale and massive government assistance enjoyed by the multinationals, Old McDonalds' farms are an endangered species. As is true of farming in America in general, when it comes to raising animals for human consumption, agribusiness has replaced agriculture.

ANIMALS AS CLOTHES

The most common justification of meat eating is that it is necessary. Every red-blooded American knows that we have to eat meat. Without three or more ample portions a day, we will not get enough protein. And without enough protein, we will end up either sick or dead. That is certainly what I was taught while I was growing up. And this is what I continued to believe well into young adulthood.

The "protein myth" ("you-have-to-eat-meat-to-get-your-protein") once enjoyed wide currency among the general public. Times have changed. Today, more and more people understand that all the protein humans need for optimal health can be obtained without eating meat (a vegetarian diet) and without eating meat or any other food derived from animals, including milk, cheese, and eggs (a vegan diet). Even the Food and Drug Administration, no friend of vegetarianism in the past, today waves a dietary flag of truce. In its most recent assessment, the FDA acknowledges that vegetarianism and veganism offer positive, healthful dietary options.

Still, one thing meat eating historically has had in its favor is its presumed necessity for achieving two very important human goods: health and survival. The same is not true in the case of another ongoing chapter in the history of human exploitation of nonhuman animals: wearing their fur. True, wearing fur might be necessary for health and survival if we are Inuits living in the far North. But in the case of people on the streets of New York? The shopping malls of Chicago or Atlanta? The ski lodges of Aspen? No, neither health nor survival explains wearing fur in these places. The reason is *fashion*. And, truth to tell, when it comes to making a fashion statement, in some circles nothing speaks louder than fur.

The number of animals utilized by the American fur industry has varied over time. Approximately 4.5 million animals were killed for fur in the United States in 2001. Mink is the most common source, accounting for roughly 80 percent of all retail fur sales.

Where does fur originate? In the not too distant past, trappers were the primary source of fur pelts, but recent years have seen a major shift in methods of procurement. Today, the majority of animals destined for the fur trade (2.5 million) are raised on what the industry calls "ranches," a word that conjures up bucolic images associated with Old McDonald's Farm, only this time for mink and other fur-bearing animals. As it happens, a "fur ranch" is as close to an actual ranch as a veal stall is to a pasture. A more appropriate name is "fur mill," since these operations produce fur-bearing animals the way steel mills produce girders.

Fur Mill Fur

Fur mills throughout the world share the same basic architecture. They consist of long rows of wire mesh cages raised several feet off the ground. The cages have a roof overhead, and a fence surrounds the entire structure. (The fence insures that any animals who happen to fall through or free themselves from their cages will not escape.) A fur mill might contain as few as one hundred or as many as one hundred thousand animals. Among the fur bearers raised are mink, chinchilla, raccoon, lynx, and foxes. For 2001 the U.S. Department of Agriculture gave 324 as the number of fur mills operating throughout the country.

Mink breeder cages, which house mothers and their kits, can contain as many as eight animals. Except for the tracks they leave behind, mink in the wild (they have a home territory up to two and one-half miles in length) are rarely seen. Nocturnal creatures, they spend most of their time in water, and their reputation for being excellent swimmers is well deserved. Confined in cages, mink are like fish out of water. Much of their waking hours finds them pacing, back and forth, back and forth, the boundaries of their diminished lives defined by the path they repeat, over and over again, in their wire mesh world.

As was noted in the discussion of veal calves, repetitive behavior of this sort is a classic symptom of psychological maladjustment. Other forms of repetitive motions (for example, jumping up the sides of cages and rotating their heads) attest to the same thing. Unnaturally confined as they are and denied an environment in which they can express their natural desires to roam and swim, fur mill mink (and we find the same behaviors in all caged fur bearers) give every appearance of being neurotic at best, psychotic at worst.

Whatever its severity, the mental state of animals in fur mills is of no direct economic concern to those who raise them. By contrast, the condition of an animal's coat is, and necessary steps are taken to preserve the coat's integrity.

For example, under the stress of close confinement, foxes in breeder cages will sometimes attack one another. Cannibalism among foxes, unknown in the wild, is not unheard of in fur mills. Proprietors respond by reducing cage density from eight to four or even two. In the worst cases, "problem" animals are destroyed.

The premium placed on not spoiling the coat carries over to the methods of killing. No throat slitting here, as is true in the case of the slaughter of veal calves. Noninvasive methods, none of which involves the use of anesthetics, are the rule. In the case of small fur bearers, mink and chinchilla in particular, a common practice is to break the animal's neck. However, because this method is labor intensive, even these small animals, as is true of many of the larger ones, frequently are asphyxiated through the use of carbon dioxide or carbon monoxide.

In some cases, anal electrocution may be the method of choice. It works this way. First a metal clamp is fastened around the animal's muzzle. Next, one end of an electrified metal rod is shoved up the animal's anus. Then a switch is turned on and the animal is electrocuted to death, "fried" from the inside out. Sometimes the procedure has to be repeated several times before the animal dies. When properly done, these methods yield unblemished pelts.

Trapping

Whereas damaged pelts do not pose a serious problem for fur mill entrepreneurs, they can be a nightmare for those who trap fur-bearing animals in the wild. The fur of these animals can be so bloody and gnarled that it is economically useless. Sometimes this "wastage" (as it is called) results because a trapped animal is attacked by a natural predator. At other times potential pelts are ruined because of the frenzied efforts of the trapped animals, as they attempt to free themselves. In other cases, trapped animals chew through their trapped leg ("wring off" in the language of trappers) before crawling away, leaving no pelt at all. Friends of Animals, which has for many years aggressively campaigned against fur, estimates that a quarter of those animals trapped for their fur (roughly 625,000) are lost to wring off. FOA literature would give us to believe that trapped animals certainly have enough time to chew themselves apart. Whatever the species, FOA estimates that these animals can spend up to a week (fifteen hours is given as the average) before they die or are killed by a trapper tending the lines.

In the United States, the steel-jawed and conibear are the most widely used traps. The conibear entraps animals by their head, neck, or upper body; the steel-jawed, by a leg. The design of the latter is simplicity itself. The steel jaws of the trap are held apart by a spring. A pressure-sensitive weight pan is baited. When the animal reaches for the bait, the spring is released and the trap slams shut.

The physical trauma a trapped animal experiences has been likened to slamming a car door on a finger. According to the animal behaviorist Desmond Morris, the shock experienced by trapped animals "is difficult for us to conceive, because it is a shock of total lack of understanding of what has happened to them. They are held, they cannot escape, their response very often is to bite at the metal with their teeth, break their teeth in the process and sometimes even chew through the leg that is being held in the trap."

Various attempts have been made to design a more "humane" trap. In place of steel jaws, for example, traps with padded jaws have been tried. None of these alternatives has caught on in the United States, and the steel-jawed leghold trap continues to be used (how often is unclear) by America's estimated 100,000 to 135,000 trappers, a third of the total number who set lines just fifteen years ago. In the fifteen nations that compose the European Union, by contrast, use of the steel-jawed leghold trap became illegal in 1995.

Whatever the type of trap used, the device itself obviously cannot distinguish between fur-bearing and nontarget animals, including ducks, birds of prey, companion animals, even humans. Trappers refer to these unintended casualties as "trash animals." Because trappers are not required to collect and report such data, hard numbers concerning "trash animals" are hard to come by. FOA estimates the total number of nontarget animals that die in traps at between four and six million annually. If we split the difference and say the number is five million, that works out to approximately fourteen thousand a day, just about ten "pieces of trash" every minute.

Semiaquatic animals, including mink and beavers, also are trapped in the wild. In their case underwater traps are common. Mink can struggle to free themselves for up to four minutes; beavers, over twenty. Eventually, the trapped animals drown. Comparatively speaking, there is very little wring off or wastage in the case of animals trapped underwater.

Whether made from milled or trapped fur-bearers, fur coats require a lot of dead animals—the smaller the animals, the more required. FOA estimates that a forty-inch fur coat requires 16 coyotes, 18 lynx, 60 mink, 45 opossums, 20 otters, 42 red foxes, 40 raccoon, 50 sables, 8 seals, 50 muskrat, or 15 beavers. Of course, the suffering and death of trapped animals used to make fur coats is only part of the story. The number of nontarget animals needs to be added; and the time trapped land animals suffer before dying (fifteen hours, as we have seen, is the FOA estimate) also should be factored in. When the necessary computations are made, a forty-inch fur coat made from coyotes, for example, equals sixteen dead coyotes, *plus* an unknown number of dead nontarget animals, *plus* more than two hundred hours of animal suffering. Similar calculations can be made for the remaining target animals. As is true of many things in life, when it comes to fur coats, there's more than meets the eye.

ANIMALS AS TOOLS

When the topic is the use of animals in science, most defenders allude to life-saving cures and other improvements in human health whose discovery, it is claimed, would have been impossible without relying on animal models. Whether the claims made on behalf of utilizing animals for this purpose are accurate or exaggerated is something about which informed people of good will can disagree. Here are two examples.

Drug manufacturers spend millions of dollars and years of research trying to develop medicines that treat diseases successfully without causing comparably bad or worse conditions ("harmful side effect") in the people taking them. Before prescription drugs are approved for public sale, federal regulations require that they be tested extensively on animals. Methodologically, the underlying assumption is that drugs that are effective and safe when given to animals will be effective and safe when taken by humans.

Everyone knows this assumption is false. The sobering and shocking news concerns how false it is. It is estimated that one hundred thousand Americans die and some two million are hospitalized annually because of the harmful side effects of the prescription drugs they are taking. That makes prescription drugs *the fourth leading cause of death* in America, behind only heart disease, cancer, and stroke. Worse, the Food and Drug Administration, the federal agency charged with regulating prescription drugs, estimates that physicians report only 1 percent of adverse drug reactions. In other words, for every adverse drug response reported, ninety-nine are not. Clearly, before vivisection's defenders can reasonably claim that human benefits greatly exceed human harms, they need honestly to acknowledge how often and how much reliance on the animal model leads to prescribed therapies that are anything but beneficial.

Massive harm to humans also is attributable to what reliance on the animal model prevents. The role of cigarette smoking in the incidence of cancer is a case in point. As early as the 1950s, human epidemiological studies revealed a causal link between cigarette smoking and lung cancer. Nevertheless, repeated efforts, made over more than fifty years, rarely succeeded in inducing tobacco-related cancers in animals. Despite the alarm sounded by public health advocates, governments around the world for decades refused to mount an educational campaign to inform smokers about the grave risks they were running. Today, one in every five deaths in the United States is attributable to the effects of smoking, and fully 60 percent of direct health care costs in the United States go to treating tobacco-related illnesses.

How much of this massive human harm could have been prevented if reliance on the animal model had not directed government health care policy? It is not clear that anyone knows the answer beyond saying, "A great deal. More than we will ever know." Once we realize how much we do not know, we might be less ready to believe that all or most lifesaving cures and other improvements in human health are due to research on animal models.

In addition to their utilization in research, animals are used in tests of household products (detergents, cleansers, polishes, and the like) and cosmetics (nail polish, shaving cream, and deodorant, for example). These tests are carried out in the name of product safety, with a view to minimizing the known risk consumers run when they use items available in the market. Some government agencies (for example, the Consumer Product Safety Commission) require that manufacturers conduct toxicity tests before their products can be legally merchandised. Requirements of this type are not universal. In many cases, toxicity tests are not legally required and, when they are, no particular test, including the LD_{50} (discussed below), is universally mandated. However, because product liability law is premised on the idea that manufacturers will do whatever is reasonably necessary to prevent consumers from running unreasonable risks, manufacturers who are not legally required to conduct toxicity tests may choose to conduct them anyway.

The LD_{50}

Throughout the past sixty years, one common toxicity test conducted on animals is the LD_{50}. "LD" stands for "lethal dose," "50" for "50 percent." As the words suggest, the LD_{50} seeks to establish at what dosage the test substance will prove lethal (that is, will kill) 50 percent of the test animals.

The LD_{50} works this way. The test substance is orally administered to the test animals, some of whom are given the substance in more, others in less, concentrated forms. In theory, anything and everything has a lethal dose. Even water has been shown to be lethal to 50 percent of test animals, if enough is consumed in a short enough period of time. In order to control variables and because the animals themselves will not "volunteer" to swallow such things as paint thinner or Christmas tree spray, a measured amount is passed through a tube and down the animals' throats. Variables are also controlled by withholding anesthetic. Anywhere from ten to sixty animals are used. Observation of their condition may last up to two weeks, during which time the requisite 50 percent normally die, after which the remaining animals are killed and their dissected bodies examined. Depending on the results, the test substance is labeled as more or less toxic if swallowed in full or diluted concentrations. Products need not be kept out of the market even if they prove to be highly toxic for test animals; instead, tests like the LD_{50} are the invisible history behind the "Harmful or fatal if swallowed" labels on cans of such items as brake fluids, household lubricants, and industrial solvents.

That manufacturers have a responsibility to inform consumers about the safety of their products is an idea no sensible person would dispute. Whether reliance on the LD_{50} test discharges this responsibility to consumers and whether using animals to discharge this responsibility is morally worth the cost to the animals are matters sensible people would do well to consider.

Scientific critics of the LD_{50}, including many who are part of the regulatory toxicity industry, find the test to be badly flawed. Results have been shown to vary from one lab to the next and even within the same lab from one day to the next. The sex, age, and diet of the test animals have been shown to skew the outcome, as has their species. Even if the results were regularly reproducible in the case of the test animals, their usefulness for humans is negligible at best. Doctors and other hospital personnel who work in emergency rooms, where the majority of accidental poisonings are dealt with, do not consult LD_{50} results before treating their patients. To suggest otherwise reflects profound ignorance of the practice of emergency medicine.

The consequences of utilizing animals in toxicity tests, when we consider the animals, are far from negligible. For them, life in a laboratory can be a living hell. In the case of LD_{50} tests, for example, animals frequently become quite ill before they die or are killed. Symptoms include diarrhea, convulsions, and bloody discharge from the mouth, eyes, and rectum. Richard Ryder, a former experimental psychologist who used animals in his research while at Cambridge and Columbia universities, characterizes the plight of animals used in LD_{50} tests of cosmetics as follows:

> Because most cosmetic products are not especially poisonous, it necessarily follows that if a rat or a dog has to be killed this way, then very great quantities of

cosmetic must be forced into their stomachs, blocking or breaking internal organs, or killing the animal by some other physical action, rather than by any specific chemical effect. Of course the procedure of force-feeding—even with healthy food—is itself a notoriously unpleasant procedure, as suffragettes and other prisoners on hunger strike have testified. When the substance forced into the stomach is not food at all, but large quantities of face powder, make up or liquid hair dye, then no doubt the suffering is very much greater indeed. If, for the bureaucratic correctness of the test, quantities great enough to kill are involved then clearly the process of dying itself must often be prolonged and agonizing.

And lest we think that, in the majority of cases, the animals used are "only rats" or "only mice," we do well to note that neither rats nor mice are classified as "animals" under the Animal Welfare Act and thus are not covered by extant federal legislation. We should also note that, unlike those animals who are covered, neither mice nor rats are able to vomit and so cannot find even the temporary relief this mechanism provides.

In response to the growing chorus of criticism, some laboratories are moving away from the LD_{50} and using "limit" tests—the LD_{10}, for example, which uses only ten animals. Whatever the number, scientific and moral questions need to be addressed. Is it scientifically credible to believe that what is discovered by using a cat or a dog, a mouse or a rat can be extrapolated to human beings? Or might it be true that the use of the animal model is a bankrupt scientific methodology? These are the basic scientific questions.

The basic moral questions are two. First, if animal model tests or research are scientifically indefensible, then how, morally, can their continued use be justified? Second, even if this methodology is scientifically defensible— indeed, even if, by relying on it, important human interests in safety and health are advanced to a degree that would be otherwise unobtainable—does that make animal model tests or research right?

The first question is explored at length in the resources cited in the notes accompanying this chapter. As for the second, it cannot be answered in a philosophical vacuum. Whether use of the animal model is right or wrong depends on general considerations about moral right and wrong. This is hardly unique to the issue at hand. Consider moral controversies that have nothing to do with animals—abortion and physician-assisted suicide, for example. Different people have deeply felt opposing views about the morality of these practices, with both sides mounting arguments in their defense. Which side is correct, is hard to say. Nevertheless, separated though they are by the judgments they make, there is one point on which all can agree: it makes sense to ask *why* people believe what they do—to ask for, and to expect to be given, *reasons* that support the moral judgments they make. If in response we are told that there *are no reasons*, the person *just knows* where the truth lies, we are wise to walk away. Our positions about controversial moral issues, whatever these positions might be, are never self-evidently true; without exception, our answers to controversial moral questions require careful, informed, fair, and well-considered rational support.

Which among the possible reasons given in support of our moral convictions really do the job—really do show that we are justified in believing what we do? When we rise to this level of inquiry, we are not asking whether an individual action or a particular practice is morally right or morally wrong. We want to know what makes *any* action or *any* practice morally right or morally wrong. This is what I meant earlier, when I said that the morality of using animals for scientific purposes cannot be assessed in a moral vacuum. To attempt to assess the morality of *this* practice necessitates asking and answering questions about the morality of *any* practice; it requires exploring the possible merits of competing moral theories. Later chapters explore some of the most influential moral theories favored by philosophers over the centuries. First, though, questions whose answers will frame our consideration of their ideas require our attention.

3

THE NATURE AND IMPORTANCE OF RIGHTS

What makes right acts right? What makes wrong acts wrong? Some moral philosophers believe that the best answers to these questions require the recognition of moral rights. This is the position I favor and the one I will try to defend. This is also a position all the moral theories examined in chapters 4 and 5, despite their many differences, unequivocally reject. It will therefore be useful to say something about the nature and importance of rights, the better to understand the work that lies ahead.

The idea of the "rights of the individual" has had a profound and lasting influence, both in and beyond Western civilization. Among philosophers, however, this idea has been the subject of intense debate. Some philosophers deny that we have any rights (moral rights, as they are commonly called) beyond those legal rights established by law; others affirm that, separate from and more basic than our legal rights, are our moral rights, including such rights as the rights to life, liberty, and bodily integrity. The framers of America's Declaration of Independence certainly believed this; they maintained that the sole reason for having a government in the first place is to protect citizens in the possession of their rights, rights that, because they are independent of and more basic than legal rights, have the status of moral rights.

POSITIVE AND NEGATIVE RIGHTS

People can agree that humans have moral rights and disagree over what rights are. They can even agree that humans have moral rights, agree about what rights are, and still disagree when it comes to saying what rights humans have. For example, some proponents of moral rights believe humans possess only *negative* moral rights (rights not to be harmed or interfered with), while others believe we also have *positive* moral rights (rights to be helped or assisted). This is an important distinction we can illustrate as follows.

Violations of Negative Moral Rights: An Example

Some people, through no fault of their own, are systematically harmed by other people. For example, teenage girls in some parts of the world are sold into conditions of abject slavery where, on a daily basis, they are beaten and sexually assaulted. If these girls have a negative right not to be harmed or interfered with, their abusers violate their rights, which is wrong. As this example suggests, negative rights are violated because of what people do to the bearers of such rights. Violations are wrongs of commission.

Violations of Positive Moral Rights: An Example

Some people, through no fault of their own, have important needs they cannot fulfill. For example, young children born into poverty are unable to pay for adequate medical care. If these children have a positive right to be helped or assisted, then those people who have the means to help have an obligation to do so. If these people fail to help, they violate the children's rights, which is wrong. As this example illustrates, positive rights are violated because of what people fail to do for the bearers of such rights. Violations are wrongs of omission.

Some philosophers (libertarians, as they are frequently called) do not believe in positive rights; for them, all moral rights are negative moral rights. Thus, while libertarians could agree that it would be a good thing for the children in the second example to receive health care, they would insist that these children do not have a right to receive it. More generally, no one has this right.

Other philosophers (those with socialist inclinations) believe in rights of both kinds; for them, some moral rights are negative, but some are positive too. Thus, because receiving health care is such an important good, these philosophers can be counted upon to argue that the children in the second example do have a right to receive it. More generally, everyone has this right.

As should be evident, these two ways of thinking about moral rights cannot both be true. If people have only negative moral rights, they cannot also have positive moral rights; and if people have positive moral rights, they cannot have only negative moral rights. So which (if either) view is correct? Both sides have presented impressive arguments. A fair, informed evaluation of the competing views would be long and difficult. Fortunately for us, these debates lie outside the scope of our present interest. Here is why.

Although the differences just remarked upon are important, so are the similarities. In fact, for our purposes, the latter are more important than the former. There is common ground among philosophers who find a place for moral rights in their moral theories. While there is disagreement over the validity of positive moral rights, there is unanimity concerning the validity of negative moral rights. For example, no advocate of human rights (at least none I know of) would brush aside the treatment of the teenage girls in the first example. Every advocate of human rights (at least everyone I know of) would see in their mistreatment a gross violation of human rights. This unanimity among these thinkers makes our work easier. For our purposes, we can table the divisive debate over positive rights for humans (the idea is broached again briefly in chapter 6) and instead concentrate on our negative moral rights. Among moral theorists in general, this is where the deep philosophical action is, the place where the fundamental questions concerning human rights arise.

The same is true concerning the debate over animal rights. The questions central to the animal rights debate also concern wrongs of commission (what people are doing to animals on factory farms and fur mills, for example). Fundamentally, what we want to know is whether the harm we visit upon them, and the freedom and life we take from them, violate their rights. As such, the central questions do not concern whether we are violating animals' rights because of wrongs of omission (for example, whether the rights of park pigeons are violated if we fail to give them an annual veterinary checkup). Questions of this latter kind are relevant certainly, and a fully developed moral theory would address them. It remains true nevertheless that questions of the former kind are more central because more fundamental.

For these reasons, our inquiry will focus on negative moral rights (henceforth "rights," for reasons of linguistic economy). What do we mean when we affirm or deny moral rights? And why is possession of them so important? These are the questions to which we now turn.

MORAL INTEGRITY: NO TRESPASSING

Possession of moral rights (by which, again, unless otherwise indicated, I mean negative moral rights) confers a distinctive moral status on those who have them. To possess these rights is to have a kind of protective moral shield, something we might picture as an invisible No Trespassing sign. If we assume that all humans have such rights, we can ask what this invisible sign prohibits. Two things, in general. First, others are not morally free to harm us; to say this is to say that, judged from the moral point of view, others are not free to take our lives or injure our bodies as they please. Second, others are not free to interfere with our free choice; to say this is to say that others are not free to limit our choices as they please. In both cases, the No Trespassing sign is meant to protect those who have rights by morally limiting the freedom of others.

Does this mean that it is always wrong to take people's lives, injure them, or restrict their freedom? Not at all. When people exceed their rights by violating ours, we act within our rights if we respond in ways that can harm or limit the freedom of the violators. For example, suppose you are attacked by a mugger; then you do nothing wrong in using physical force sufficient to defend yourself, even if this harms your assailant. Thankfully, in the world as we find it, such cases are the exception, not the rule. Most people most of the time act in ways that respect the rights of other human beings. But even if the world happened to be different in this respect, the central point would be the same: what we are free to do when someone violates our rights does not translate into an unrestricted freedom to violate theirs.

MORAL WEIGHT: TRUMP

Every serious advocate of human rights believes that our rights have greater moral weight than other important human values. To use an analogy from the card game bridge, our moral rights are trump. Here is what this analogy means.

A hand is dealt. Hearts are trump. The first three cards played are the queen of spades, the king of spades, and the ace of spades. You (the last player) have no spades. However, you do have the two of hearts. Because hearts are trump, your lowly two of hearts beats the queen of spades, beats the king of spades, even beats the ace of spades. This is how powerful the trump suit is in the game of bridge.

The analogy between trump in bridge and individual rights in morality should be reasonably clear. There are many important values to consider when we make a moral decision. For example: How will we be affected personally as a result of deciding one way or another? What about our family, friends, neighbors, fellow Americans? It is not hard to write a long list. When we say, "rights are trump," we mean that respect for the rights of individuals is the most important consideration in "the game of morality," so to speak. In particular, we mean that the good others derive from violating someone's rights (by injuring their bodies or taking their lives, for example) never justifies violating them.

MORAL STATUS: EQUALITY

Moral rights breathe equality. They are the same for all who have them, differ though we do in many ways. This explains why no human being can justifiably be denied rights for arbitrary, prejudicial, or morally irrelevant reasons. Race is such a reason. To attempt to determine which humans have rights on the basis of race is like trying to sweeten tea by adding salt. What race we are tells us nothing about what rights we have.

The same is no less true of other differences between us. Nancy and I trace our family lineage to different countries—she to Lithuania, I to Ireland. Some of our friends are Christians, some Jews, and some Moslems. Others are agnostics or atheists. In the world at large, a few people are very wealthy, many more, very poor. And so it goes. Humans differ in many ways. There is no denying that.

Still, no one who believes in human rights thinks these differences mark fundamental moral divisions. If we mean anything by the idea of human rights, we mean that we *have them equally*. And we have them equally (if we have them at all) regardless of our race, gender, religious belief, comparative wealth, intelligence, or date or place of birth, for example.

MORAL CLAIMS: JUSTICE

Rights involve justice, not generosity; what we are due, not what we want. Here is an example that helps illustrate the difference. I happen to want a fancy sports car, which I cannot afford. Bill Gates (as everyone knows) has more money than he knows what to do with. I write to him:

Dear Bill:
    I want an Audi TT 3.2-litre six-cylinder sports coupe with a direct shift gearbox. I can't afford the asking price. I know you can. So I would appreciate

it if you would send me a money order (by Express Mail, if you don't mind) to
cover the cost.

Your new friend,
Tom

One thing is abundantly clear. I am not in a position to demand that Bill
Gates buy me an Audi TT. Receiving a car from him—any car—is not something to which I am entitled, not something I am owed or due. If my new-
found friend Bill bought me the car of my dreams, his gift would distinguish
him as uncommonly generous (or uncommonly foolish), not uncommonly
fair.

When we invoke our rights, by contrast, we are not asking for anyone's
generosity. We are not saying, "Please, will you kindly give me something I
do not deserve?" On the contrary, when we invoke our rights, we are demanding fair treatment, demanding that we receive what is our due. We are not
asking for any favors.

MORAL RIGHTS: VALID CLAIMS

The preceding discussion helps explain the general characterization of rights
as valid claims, an analysis of rights that is pervasive throughout the animal
rights debate (for example, this is the analysis favored by Carl Cohen, the
most influential critic of animal rights) and the one I will use throughout
these pages. To say that rights are claims means that rights represent treatment
that one is justified in demanding, treatment that is strictly owed, either for
oneself or for others. To say that such a claim is valid means that the claim is
rationally justified. Thus, whether a claim to a right is valid depends on
whether the basis of the claim is justified. A question of great importance (to
understate the case) asks: What justifies such claims?

The answer I will be defending ties the validity of claims to valid principles
of direct duty. For example, our claim to a right to life is valid if others have
a direct duty not to take our lives as they please (that is, if the duty not to take
life is a valid principle of direct duty), and our claim to a right to liberty is
valid if others have a direct duty not to interfere with our liberty as they please
(that is, if the duty not to interfere is a valid principle of direct duty). Obviously, this explanation itself stands in need of explanation. In particular,
something clearly needs to be said about "direct duties." And something
more will be said about this and related ideas in the following chapters. We

revisit the analysis of rights as valid claims in chapter 6, in the discussion of human rights, and in chapter 8, in the examination of Cohen's objections to animal rights. Before ending this chapter, one final idea requires our attention.

MORAL UNITY: RESPECT

Trespass. Trump. Equality. Justice. These are among the ideas that come to the surface when we review the meaning and importance of moral rights. While each is essential, none succeeds in unifying the core concept. By contrast, the idea of respect succeeds in doing this.

The rights discussed in this chapter (life, liberty, and bodily integrity) are variations on a main theme, that theme being respect. From the perspective of human rights proponents, I show my respect for you by respecting these rights in your life, and you show your respect for me by doing the same thing in my life. Respect is the main theme because treating one another with respect *just is* treating one another in ways that respect our other rights. From this perspective, our most fundamental right, the right that unifies all our other rights, is our right to be treated with respect. When our other rights are violated, we are treated with a lack of respect.

ANIMAL RIGHTS?

It is when viewed against this larger moral backdrop that the importance of the debate over animal rights comes into sharper focus. *If* animals have rights of the sort mentioned (the rights to bodily integrity and to life, for example), then the way they are treated on farms and in biomedical research violates their rights, is wrong, and should be stopped, no matter how much humans have benefited from these practices in the past or how much we might benefit from having them continue in the future.

Philosophical opponents of animal rights agree. "[I]f animals have any rights at all," writes Cohen, "they have the right to be respected, the right not to be used as a tool to advance human interests . . . no matter how important those human interests are thought to be." In particular, if nonhuman animals have moral rights, biomedical research that uses them is wrong and should be stopped. Cohen even goes so far as to liken the use of animals, in the development of the polio and other vaccines, to the use Nazi scientists made of Jewish children during the Second World War. "[I]f those animals we used and continue to use have rights as human children do, what we did and are doing to them is as profoundly wrong as what the Nazis did to those Jews not long ago."

Clearly, what is true of the morality of relying on the animal model in scientific research would be no less true when evaluating the morality of commercial animal agriculture and the fur trade. These, too, would be "profoundly wrong," if animals have rights. On this point, without a doubt, even Cohen would agree.

But *do* animals have rights? More fundamentally, do *human beings* have rights? These are among the central questions to be addressed in the pages that follow. At this juncture I note only that my argument for animal rights cannot be made in twenty-five words or less. Why animals have rights can be understood only after critically examining moral theories that deny rights to animals and, sometimes, to humans, too. Once we understand the weaknesses of these theories, we can understand why human rights must be acknowledged; and once we adopt this latter position, then—but not before, in my judgment—we can understand why we must acknowledge animal rights as well.

In the nature of the case, therefore, as I indicated earlier and as I will have occasion to say again, my argument for animal rights is cumulative in nature, arising as it does in response to weaknesses in other ways of thinking about morality. What these other ways are, where some of their weaknesses lie, are explored in the following pages.

4

INDIRECT DUTY VIEWS

M ost people like animals. Very few are indifferent to their suffering, and fewer still would intentionally mistreat a cat, dog, or any animal for that matter. When children torment a puppy or kitten, most parents and other grown-ups are quick to reprimand them. We want our children to empathize with, not be the cause of, another's pain. For many children, one of life's earliest lessons in empathy concerns the suffering of animals.

But while almost all of us are of one mind when it comes to opposing the mistreatment of animals, most people evidently believe we do nothing wrong when we make them suffer or die in pursuit of various human interests. At least this is the verdict supported by the behavior and judgments of the majority of Americans. According to recent polls, somewhere in the neighborhood of 98 percent eat meat; a clear majority (70 percent) approves of using animals to test medical treatments; and the public is divided when it comes to wearing fur (50 percent against, 35 percent for, and 15 percent undecided). How is it possible for people to oppose mistreating animals and, at the same time, to support practices they know cause animals pain and involve deliberately killing them?

Moral philosophers, as well as other people of conscience, are not short on possible answers. One influential explanation favored by some philosophers grants that we have duties *involving* animals but denies that we have any duties *to* them. It will be useful to give a name to moral theories of this type. For reasons that will become clearer as we proceed, I refer to them as indirect duty views. The present chapter examines two views of this type (simple and Rawlsian contractarianism) and explains why, in the end, despite the important contributions they make, all indirect duty views are and must be unsatisfactory.

An example should help clarify the basic logic of indirect duty views. Suppose you share your life with a dog, whom you love dearly. Your next-door neighbor does not share your affection. He regards your dog as a nuisance and makes no effort to conceal his feelings. One day, without provocation, you see him deliberately break her leg. Proponents of indirect duty views will agree that your neighbor has done something wrong. But not to your dog. The wrong that has been done, they will say, is a wrong to you. After all, it is wrong to upset people and, by injuring your dog, your neighbor has upset you. So *you* are the one who is wronged, *not* your dog. Or again: by breaking your dog's leg, your neighbor damages your property. Since it is wrong to damage another person's property, your neighbor has done something wrong—to you, that is, not to your dog. Your neighbor no more wrongs your dog by breaking her leg than he would wrong your clock if he broke its hands.

While all indirect duty views deny that we have duties to animals, there is room for disagreement concerning why this is so. People who accept indirect duty views might deny direct duties to nonhuman animals because these animals are not created in the image of God, for example, or because animals, unlike us, are not able to use abstract principles when they make decisions. When we classify a position as an indirect duty view, therefore, we leave important moral questions open. What makes right acts right and what makes wrong acts wrong remain to be explained, and the explanation given will depend on the particulars of the indirect duty view being reviewed. One basis common to a variety of indirect duty views involves the idea of interests. Because this idea plays a central role in all the moral theories I will be discussing, it will be useful to say something more about it here.

TWO KINDS OF INTERESTS

The interests people have are of two kinds. Preference interests refer to what people are *interested in*, what they want to do or possess. Interests of this kind often differ greatly between different individuals. For example, some people would rather golf than play tennis; some prefer the opposite; and others, liking neither, would rather curl up with a book or spend their free time surfing the Internet. People also differ when it comes to the things they want. For example, some people are not satisfied unless they have closets full of clothes, while others think having the basics is enough. The preferences we have not only help define who we are, they also help describe how we differ.

Welfare interests are conceptually distinct from preference interests. Welfare interests refer to what is *in our interests*, including those things and conditions that are necessary if we are to have a minimally satisfactory existence, both physically and psychologically. Food, shelter, and health are welfare interests we all share, differ though we do when it comes to our preference interests. Logic suggests, and experience confirms, that the two sorts of interests can conflict, sometimes with tragic consequences. For example, people with serious drug problems can ruin their lives by sacrificing their most important welfare interests in pursuit of the preference interests that define their addiction.

Some advocates of indirect duty views deny that we have duties directly to animals because of how they understand human and animal interests. The interests animals have, if in fact they have any, it is claimed, are of no direct relevance to morality, whereas human interests, meaning both our preference interests and our welfare interests, are directly relevant. Because we cannot have direct duties to those whose interests are not directly relevant to morality, this way of viewing interests yields the conclusion that we do not have direct duties to animals. This in turn would explain why your neighbor did not violate a duty he owed to your dog. Because your dog's interest in avoiding pain, assuming she has this interest, is of no direct moral relevance, your neighbor's hurting her is not directly morally relevant, either. That being so, the idea of your neighbor's having a duty directly to your dog and, in general, the idea of any human being having a duty directly to any animal being, emerge as morally empty

Why would anyone think that animal interests have no direct relevance to morality? If your dog suffers because your neighbor has broken her leg, how could any rational person deny that her pain is directly morally relevant? Logic suggests, and this time history confirms, that one way to defend this position is to deny that nonhuman animals feel anything, pain included. That such a proposal goes against the grain of common sense is too obvious to require proof. Still, as is famously said, common sense tells us the world is flat. So perhaps we are just as mistaken about what animals experience as flat-earthers are about the shape of our planet. Remarkably, some philosophers think we are.

CARTESIANISM THEN AND NOW

As was just noted, one way to support an indirect duty view is to deny that animals are aware of anything. It is important to grasp the full meaning of what is being proposed. We are not being asked to believe that nonhuman animals experience the same things we do only less intensely; or that they experience different things than we do that we cannot begin to understand or even imagine; instead, we are being asked to believe that animals do not experience anything at all, that their mental lives are totally nonexistent. Given such a view, animals are as mindless as wristwatches, and questions about how they should be treated are on a par with asking about my duty to your Timex. From the moral point of view, we do not have duties *to* animals, just as we do not have duties *to* watches; rather, we have duties to humans that sometimes involve animals and watches.

Now, there was a time, owing to the influence of the seventeenth-century French philosopher René Descartes, when many scientists enthusiastically embraced the view that nonhuman animals are mindless, totally devoid of any conscious experience. Nicholas Fontaine, a contemporary of Descartes, captures the reigning ideology of the times in these words:

> The [Cartesian] scientists administered beatings to dogs with perfect indifference and made fun of those who pitied the creatures as if they felt pain. They said the animals were clocks; that the cries they emitted when struck were only the noise of a little spring that had been touched, but that the whole body was without feeling. They nailed the poor animals up on boards by their four paws to vivisect them to see the circulation of the blood which was a subject of great controversy.

Descartes offers several arguments to support his view that animals are not aware of anything, the most important of which deals with the ability to use language. We humans learn about one another's mental lives because we are able to communicate. I describe what I see and hear and feel; you do the same in your case. Unlike us, animals are unable to do this. Because they lack the ability to use a language such as French or English, Descartes maintains that animals offer no compelling evidence that they are aware of anything. And because they fail to offer such evidence, Descartes concludes that animals lack any sort of mental life. Animals are (to use his words) "nature's machines," bodies without minds, biological wind-up toys as lacking in mental awareness as the Energizer Bunny.

Descartes's views are so patently at odds with common sense that they have attracted few adherents over the last three centuries. It may therefore come as a surprise to learn that the past several years have witnessed a minor renaissance of the Cartesian denial of animal awareness. The English philosopher Peter Carruthers is representative of the neo-Cartesians. Following in Descartes's footsteps, Carruthers argues that because animals are unable to use language, they are unable to think, and because they are unable to think, they are not conscious of anything. Notwithstanding the fact that a coyote caught in a steel-jawed leghold trap behaves as if she suffers terribly, the animal has no interest in avoiding what she does not experience. In Carruthers's view, animal pain is "unconscious."

Descartes's and Carruthers's language argument for denying conscious experience to nonhuman animals will not stand up under logical scrutiny. Consider this: Human children *must* be aware of things before they learn to use a language. If they were not, if they could neither see nor hear nor feel prior to learning to talk, they could never learn to talk. There would be no point—there *could* be no point—in holding up the cat and, while pointing, saying "kitty," if preverbal children were unable to see the cat or hear our voices. Human children *must* be preverbally (and thus *nonverbally*) aware of the world if they are to become linguistically proficient. This last point is crucial. Unless matters are prejudged arbitrarily, once we concede the reality of nonverbal awareness in humans, we cannot summarily deny nonverbal awareness in animals. Of course, only a very few people out of the many billions who have lived have denied mental awareness to nonhuman animals; only a very small minority have claimed that these animals, like wristwatches, have no interests. The Cartesian's ability to suspend belief to the contrary, the rest of us are people of common sense, people who recognize our psychological kinship with other animals. Like us, many animals (which ones is a question I take up below) have both preference interests and welfare interests. Some things they want to have or do; others they want to avoid or escape. And some things (food, water, shelter, for example) are no less essential for them, if they are to have a minimally satisfying life, than they are for us.

SCIENCE AND ANIMAL MINDS

But it is not just common sense that declares that many other animals are our psychological kin. Our best science supports the same conclusion. Darwin sees this clearly in the case of evolutionary theory. *Naturam non facit saltum* (nature does not make jumps) is central to his understanding of how existing species of life, including the human, have come into being. Evolutionary theory teaches that what is more mentally complex evolves from what is less mentally complex, not that what is more mentally complex, the human mind in particular, springs full-blown from what lacks mind altogether. If that were true, nature would make some very big jumps indeed. Viewed in evolutionary terms, other-than-human minds populate the nonhuman world.

Darwin's teachings find support in comparative anatomy and physiology. Human anatomy and physiology are not in every way unique. On the contrary, as Darwin observes, "man bears in his bodily structure clear traces of descent from" other species of animals. These similarities of structure and function in the anatomy and physiology of humans and other animals are too obvious to be denied, their importance too great to be ignored. Thus may we ask, in the words of the seventeenth-century French philosopher Voltaire in his sarcastic rejection of Cartesianism: "Has nature arranged all the means of feeling in the animal, so that it may not feel? . . . Do not suppose this impertinent contradiction in nature."

On this matter, Darwin sides with Voltaire. Vast numbers of other-than-human-animals have mental lives, have a psychology. Writing of mammalian animals, Darwin observes that "[t]here is no fundamental difference between man and the higher animals in their mental faculties." The difference in the mental life of human beings and other mammals, he adds, is "one of degree, not of kind."

What Darwin means, I think, is that these animals are like us in having a rich, unified mental life. Darwin himself catalogs the mental attributes he finds in other mammals, basing his findings on his own and others' observations of their behavior. It is an impressive list, including (in addition to the capacity to experience pleasure and pain [sentiency]) such emotions as terror, suspicion, courage, rage, shame, jealousy, grief, love, and affection, and such higher order cognitive abilities as curiosity, attention, memory, imagination, and reason.

For Darwin, there is nothing the least bit irrational or antiscientific in the belief that coyotes and veal calves prefer some things over others; that some things are in their interests (that is, contribute to their experiential welfare); or that they remember events from the past, anticipate what will happen in the future, and are able to act deliberately, with the intention of satisfying their preferences in the future. It is only when we ask *how much* they remember or anticipate, or *how many things* they want to have and do, that differences emerge.

Our knowledge of the past, for example, extends beyond the limits of our own experience. The life of Plato. The fall of Rome. The Lisbon earthquake. The forced internment of Japanese Americans during the Second World War. No animal other than the human has such knowledge, just as no animal other than the human worries about the stock market, rejoices in a Steeler victory, or (to quote Darwin again) is able to "follow out a train of metaphysical reasoning, solve a mathematics problem, or reflect on God." Even so, there is sameness beneath the differences. In many important respects, though of course not in all, the mental lives of humans and other animals are fundamentally similar.

The considerations that support viewing mammalian animals as having mental lives do not exclude the possibility that the same thing is true of animals of other kinds. For example, it is hard to understand how birds would fail to qualify. Recent studies from throughout the world demonstrate diverse avian cognitive abilities. These include the abilities to learn from experience, to teach conspecifics, to reason logically, and to adjust behavior if observed by others. For example, scrub jays will return, alone, to move food to a new place if other scrub jays were watching where they hid it originally.

Do birds have interests? Are there some things they want to have or do, others that they want to escape or avoid? Do some conditions contribute to their experiential welfare—to whether their lives go well or ill for them? The onus of proof must surely be borne by those who would give a negative answer to any of these questions.

Should we go further? Should we say that all vertebrates, including fish, have interests? A psychology? A mind? The basis for including fish is not weak by any means. Like humans, fish have a complicated physiology, anatomy, brain, and spinal chord. In addition, they have highly developed nerve endings near the surface of their bodies, especially near their mouths. In the spirit of Voltaire, would it not be an odd quirk of biology to provide fish with all the means of feeling pain and then deny the feeling? This is not runaway anthropomorphism. Thelma Lee Gross, DVM, summarizing current knowledge, states that "[d]irect clinical experience and scientific research has led [experts who work with fish] to realize that these animals feel pain."

Other experts have shown that fish who live in stable groups ("families") recognize each other, either by sight or sound. They can remember how conspecifics behaved in the past and alter their own behavior accordingly. The range of fish memory extends to features of the environment, including recognition of territories or home ranges. In other words, fish know where they are and where they are going. Older fish teach younger fish what to eat and what to avoid, and fish of any age can learn where to find food by observing the behavior of other fish. Moreover, fish have demonstrated what cognitive ethologists call associative reasoning, or the ability to take what was learned in the past and apply it to novel situations in the future. Do fish have interests? Is there somebody there, behind those unblinking eyes?

Some people, I am sure, will think we go too far when we attribute much by way of mental complexity to fish or other vertebrates. We will be told that their brains are too primitive, their central nervous system too rudimentary, to carry such heavy psychological baggage. Good sense should prevail. We need to "draw the line" at a place on the phylogenetic scale that excludes fish and other vertebrates.

Well, perhaps. Then again, perhaps not. While it should be clear where my sympathies lie, for the sake of argument I am prepared to limit the conclusions for which I argue to the *least controversial* cases, by which I mean mammals and birds. (I say the "least controversial" because, as we have seen, some philosophers argue that all nonhuman animals, including mammals and birds, are mindless).The grounds for attributing interests and, with this, a psychology to these animal beings are analogous to those we have for attributing minds to one another. Common sense supports it. How they behave supports it. Their physiology and anatomy support it. And their having interests, their having a psychology, is supported by well-established scientific principles. Not one of these considerations by itself need be claimed as "proof" of animal minds; it is when they are taken together that they provide compelling grounds for attributing a mental life to other than human animals.

We may conclude, therefore, that our common sense belief in animal minds has good reasons on its side. Sheep and hogs, mink and beavers, owls and ravens, for example, are psychologically present in and to the world, with mental lives that, while not as complex as ours, are not simple by any means. In particular, like us, they have both preference interests and welfare interests. Any plausible account of the moral status of animals must be consistent with the convictions of common sense, bolstered by the findings of an informed science.

One last point before proceeding: Many people of good will do not believe in evolution. They believe that human existence is the result of a special creation by God, something that took place approximately ten thousand years ago. For these people, the evidence for animal minds provided by evolutionary theory is no evidence at all. Despite first impressions, the rejection of evolution need not undermine the main conclusions summarized in the previous paragraph. All of the world's religions speak with one voice when it comes to the question before us. None speaks in the vocabulary of the Cartesian. Read the Bible, the Torah, the Koran. Study Confucianism, Buddhism, Hinduism, or Native American spiritual writings. The message is everywhere the same. Mammals and birds *most certainly* are psychologically present in and to the world. These animals *most certainly* have both preference and welfare interests. In these respects, all the world's religions teach the same thing.

Thus, while the argument I have given appeals to the implications of evolutionary theory, the conclusions I reach are entirely consistent with the religion-based convictions of people who do not believe in evolution. And for those who believe both in God and in evolution? Well, these people have reasons of both kinds for recognizing the minds of the other animals with whom we share a common habitat: the earth. I will have more to say about religion and animals in chapter 8.

SIMPLE CONTRACTARIANISM

For the most part (Carruthers being among the few exceptions), contemporary philosophers who hold indirect duty views grant that the animals we have been considering have various experiences, including some that are painful, others pleasant. In other words, most indirect duty theorists are not Cartesians. How do these philosophers justify their position? Among this question's most influential replies are those favored by philosophers known as contractarians.

Here is the basic idea. When two people negotiate a contract, both parties seek to advance or protect their individual self-interest. Contracts are entered into for the good of each person who signs, and no one should sign unless convinced that it is to that person's advantage to do so.

For contractarians, morality shares these essential features of contracting. From a contractarian perspective, morality consists of a set of rules that all the contractors should follow because doing so is in each contractor's rational self-interest. For example, contractors might recognize that it is to their personal advantage to limit their freedom in order to increase their security. I agree not to steal your things if you agree not to steal mine; each of us voluntarily surrenders some of our freedom, but both of us reap the benefit of added security.

What makes right acts right? What makes wrong acts wrong? Contractarian answers generalize on the example of theft. Acts are right if they conform to a valid rule, wrong if they fail to conform to (if they break) a valid rule, the validity of the rules to be determined by the self-interest of the contractors. Valid rules are rules that advance the rational self-interest of the contractors if everyone who participates in framing the contract follows them.

It is important to recognize why, according to this form of contractarianism, referred to here as "simple contractarianism," the contractors enjoy a moral status that many humans lack. The interests of those who take part in framing the contract are directly morally relevant because their interests form the basis of the contract; this is why the framers are owed direct duties. By contrast, the interests of those who do not take part in framing the contract, because their interests do not form the basis of the contract, are not directly morally relevant; this is why no direct duties are owed in their case. This difference means a lot if you are a young child, for example. Because young children are unable to discern what is in their rational self-interest, they cannot participate in framing the contract; thus, *their* interests are not directly morally relevant; in their case, therefore, no direct duties are owed. Does this mean that contractors are morally free to treat children any way they please? Not necessarily. If the contractors have self-interested reasons in seeing that their own children are well treated (for example, because they will want their children to look after them in old age), we can understand why rational, self-interested contractors would include rules that require that children should be well treated. There would thus be duties *involving* children, but no duties *to* them. Our duties in their case result from the direct duties we owe to the rational, self-interested persons who devise the contract.

As for animals, since they cannot understand contracts, they cannot participate. Accordingly, what interests they have are not directly relevant to morality. This much granted, the conclusion that they are not owed direct duties comes as no surprise. Still, like children, some animals are the objects of the sentimental interests of others. Those animals whom enough contractors care about (cats, dogs, whales, baby seals), though they will not be owed any direct duties, will have some indirect protection. For example, there might be a rule against eating cats and dogs because contractors find this practice upsetting and another rule that protects baby seals because contractors find them adorable. In the case of other animals, where no or little sentimental interest is present—the millions of rodents used in laboratories and the billions of chickens slaughtered to be eaten, for example—what indirect duties there are grow weaker and weaker, perhaps to vanishing point. The pain and death these animals endure, though real, are not wrong if no one cares about them.

Simple contractarianism's position regarding moral standing is straightforward. Who counts morally? Those individuals who participate in framing the contract. Who does not count morally? Those individuals who do not participate in framing the contract. Thus, nonhuman animals, no matter how much they are like contractors psychologically, do not have moral standing. The same is true of all those human beings (young children, for example) who lack the capacities presupposed by the ability to enter into contracts. In fact, as we shall see momentarily, *even humans who have these capacities* can lack moral standing, given the tenets of simple contractarianism. This does not bode well for the simple contractarian.

Evaluating Simple Contractarianism

Simple contractarianism has its attractions. Because it emphasizes a central role for reason in the determination of moral right and wrong, it distances itself from views that reduce morality to our unreflective feelings and from outlooks that equate what is right and wrong with the reigning customs of the society into which we happen to be born. These are among simple contractarianism's strengths. As for its weaknesses, only two will be noted here. The first concerns how the position distorts the notion of justice; the second traces some of the morally unacceptable implications this distortion allows.

Concerning the matter of distortion: Morality, the simple contractarian tells us, consists of rules that rational, self-interested people agree to follow. Which people? Well, those who create the contract. This is all well and good for those who participate in framing the rules, but not so well and good for those who are excluded. And there is nothing in simple contractarianism—let me repeat this, as a point of emphasis—there is nothing in simple contractarianism that explains why it would be wrong to exclude some rationally competent human beings from participating in the formulation of the contract. Only a gross distortion of elementary justice would allow this.

To make this distortion clearer, consider what elementary justice requires. Elementary justice requires that we treat everyone fairly, not giving to some people more than they deserve, not withholding from others that to which they are entitled. In the case of welfare interests, for example, if my interest in having access to food and shelter is equal to your interest in having access to food and shelter, then, assuming that morality is based on interests and that other things are equal, it would be unfair to count my interests as being of greater importance than yours. Equal interests count equally. So says the voice of elementary justice, of fairness, when applied to interests.

Simple contractarianism is not bound by elementary justice. Because what is just and unjust and fair and unfair is *what the contractors decide*, the interests of some people might be ignored altogether, while the interests of others might be given much greater weight or importance. For this reason alone, simple contractarianism cannot claim our rational assent.

But it is not for this reason alone that simple contractarianism should be rejected. The distortion of justice just noted (and here I turn to my second criticism) has morally unacceptable implications; this becomes clear when we ask which people might be denied the opportunity to participate in framing the moral contract. In the nature of the case, they would be people the contractors have self-interested reasons to exclude. An obvious candidate would be a racial minority whose members would best serve the contractors' interests if, say, those in the minority were bought and sold, and forced to perform slave labor. And the same could be true of other people who belong to other vulnerable groups (for example, those who are physically disadvantaged or mentally impaired), provided the contractors have self-interested reasons to exclude and exploit them.

As should be evident from these examples, simple contractarianism can have alarming implications, sanctioning the most blatant forms of social, economic, moral, and political injustice, ranging from a repressive caste system to systematic racial or gender discrimination. Let those who are not covered by the contract suffer as they will; it matters not so long as the contractors have decided that the suffering of "outsiders" does not matter morally. Such an outlook takes one's moral breath away . . . as if, for example, there would be nothing wrong with enslaving an African American minority if the moral contract was drawn up by a majority of bigoted whites. Wherever the truth might lie, there must be a better moral theory than this one.

Simple contractarianism's implications for animal beings, we know, are both clear and unsurprising. Because they lack the requisite abilities to participate in framing the contract, contractors have no direct duties to them. Indeed, the interests of animals are not in any way directly morally relevant and, if the contractors decide to do so, can be ignored completely. Elementary justice can therefore be transgressed just as easily in the case of nonhuman animals as it can be in the case of humans.

Is this a satisfactory way to think of our moral ties to other animals? Would we be justified in using simple contractarianism as a basis for excluding animals or their interests from moral consideration? It is difficult to see how this could be reasonable. A moral theory that has so little to recommend it when it comes to how other humans may be treated would seem to provide a very poor basis for evaluating our treatment of other animals. In particular, a moral theory that implies that some human beings may be treated as chattel offers no good reason to make chattel of animal beings, either. Any credible moral theory will have to do better than this.

RAWLSIAN CONTRACTARIANISM

The version of contractarianism just examined is, confessedly, a simple variety, and in fairness to those of a contractarian persuasion, it needs to be said that more refined, subtle, and ingenious varieties are possible. For example, the late John Rawls, in his monumental *A Theory of Justice*, sets forth a strikingly original interpretation of contractarianism. As is true of simple contractarianism, Rawls's version denies that we have any direct duties to animals; but unlike simple contractarianism, his position arguably will not sanction prejudicial discrimination of humans based on race or gender or permit evil institutions such as chattel slavery. Here is why.

As would-be contractors, Rawls invites us to ignore those characteristics that make us different—such characteristics as our race and class, intelligence and skills, even our date of birth and where we live. We are to imagine that our knowledge of such personal details is hidden from us by what Rawls calls a "veil of ignorance." Rawls describes our situation in these words:

> No one knows his place in society, his class position or social status, nor does anyone know his fortune in the distribution of natural assets and abilities, his intelligence, strength and alike. I shall even assume that the parties do not know their conceptions of the good or their special psychological propensities. To [choose] the principles of justice [from] behind a veil of ignorance . . . insures that no one is advantaged or disadvantaged in the choice of principles by the outcome of natural chance or the contingency of social circumstances. Since all are similarly situated and no one is able to design principles to favor his particular condition, the principles of justice are the result of a fair agreement or bargain.

Despite our ignorance of such details, Rawls does allow us to know that we will someday be members of a community whose basic rules of justice we are being asked to formulate. All that is required to participate is that we have "a sense of justice," understood as a "normally effective desire to apply and act on the principles of justice, at least to a minimum degree." Or, alternatively (for Rawls describes the qualifying conditions in another way), those who participate must have the "ability to understand and act upon whatever principles are adopted."

What rules or principles contractors would select from behind the veil of ignorance is less important for our purposes than the procedure by which they make their selection. Rawls's procedure is clearly superior to the one favored by simple contractarianism, something we can appreciate if we reconsider the two objections raised against that view. Recall, first, how simple contractarianism distorts the idea of elementary justice by permitting the contractors to assign much greater importance to their interests than they assign to the equal interests of those who are denied the opportunity to participate in framing the contract. Rawlsian contractarianism arguably will not allow this. Because contractors do not know *who they will be*, they will want to make sure that *everyone's* interests are taken into account and counted equitably. To be satisfied with anything less would be to fail to look out for one's self-interest, *whosoever* one happens to be. In this respect, Rawls's version of contractarianism is superior to the simple variety.

Rawls also has a reply to the second objection, the one that noted how simple contractarianism has morally unacceptable implications, allowing, as it does, the systematic exploitation of those not covered by the contract, members of a racial minority being an obvious example. Rawlsian contractors arguably would not permit this. Positioned as they are behind the veil of ignorance, contractors cannot know what race they will be; as such, whether they will belong to the majority race or to a racial minority is something they do not know. Lacking such knowledge, the rational choice for self-interested contractors to make is arguably one that guarantees that no group of people, including those who belong to a racial minority, will be exploited. After all, for all the contractors know, the minority race could turn out to be *their* race. Once again, therefore, the Rawlsian contractarianism is arguably superior to what I have been calling the simple version.

Though Rawls focuses on justice in particular, he notes that the procedure he favors "hold(s) for the choice of all ethical principles and not only for those of justice." Seen in this light, the same language used to characterize simple contractarianism can be used to describe the Rawlsian variety. Acts are right if they conform to a valid rule, wrong if they fail to conform to (if they break) a valid rule, the validity of the rules to be determined by asking whether the self-interest of rational contractors is advanced by having everyone obey them. Where Rawls's position differs procedurally from simple contractarianism, as has already been noted, is over *how* the rules are selected and, to some degree, regarding *who* gets to participate in the selection process.

Evaluating Rawlsian Contractarianism

Rawls's "veil of ignorance" has received a good deal of criticism at the hands of some philosophers. Whether this criticism is well founded or not, the "veil of ignorance" arguably helps illuminate one way to think about what is just and fair. Because we are selecting principles of justice from the point of view of our rational self-interest, to know that we will be white and male, for example, will give us powerful self-interested reasons to select principles that give the interests of white men a privileged moral status. However, fairness should be color- and gender-blind. From the point of view of justice, the interests of some people should not be ignored because of facts about their race or gender, nor should their interests be counted for less than the like interests of others. To assign a privileged moral status to the interests of some people and, implicitly, to assign a lower status to the comparable interests of others, based solely on considerations about race or gender, are classic expressions of two of the worst forms of prejudice: racism in the one case, sexism in the other. Rawls's "veil of ignorance" is designed to prevent these and other prejudices from having an undue influence in the selection of principles of justice.

But while Rawlsian contractarianism arguably denies the moral legitimacy of some of the worst prejudices, it is not entirely free of prejudicial implications. In Rawls's view, we have direct duties only to those humans who have "a sense of justice," understood as a "normally effective desire to apply and act on the principles of justice, at least to a minimum degree." Human infants as well as seriously mentally disadvantaged human beings of all ages do not satisfy this requirement. Even if we recognize their mental capacities (for example, sentiency, perceptual awareness, memory, and various emotions), there is no basis for crediting them with a "sense of justice," in Rawls's sense. In this respect, therefore, Rawlsian contractarianism is indistinguishable from simple contractarianism: both deny that we owe direct duties to these human beings. And in both cases, therefore, another moral prejudice is detectable, only this one a yet-to-be-named prejudice against the most vulnerable members of the extended human family.

The following example highlights the prejudice I have in mind. Suppose a mugger has pushed you to the ground and stolen your money; you are left with a number of cuts and bruises—minor, to be sure, but still painful. Alongside your condition, consider the following testimony presented by Issac Parker before Great Britain's House of Commons Select Committee. The year is 1790. The matter before the Committee, the Atlantic slave trade. Parker describes the following episode involving a sick child, who would not eat, and a Captain Marshall, who was determined to make him do so:

> The child took sulk and would not eat . . . [T]he captain took the child up in his hand and flogged it with the cat . . . [T]he child had swelled feet; the captain desired the cook to put on some hot water to heat to see if he could abate the swelling, and it was done. He then ordered the child's feet to be put into the water, and the cook putting his finger into the water said, "Sir, it is too hot." The captain said, "Damn it, never mind it, put the feet in," and so doing

the skin and nails came off. . . . I gave the child some victuals, but it would not eat; the captain took the child up again, and flogged it, and said, "Damn you, I will make you eat," and so he continued that way for four or five days at mess time. . . . The last time he took the child up and flogged it, and let it drop out of his hands, "Damn you [says he] I will make you eat, or I will be the death of you," and in three quarters of an hour after that the child died.

Death for this poor child surely was a merciful release from the all but unimaginable pain endured. When we learn that the object of Captain Marshall's abuse was all of *nine months old*, we are (if we are normal) sickened to the core. The depths of depravity to which we humans can sink never ceases to shock. And never should.

So here we have the two cases: your relatively minor pain caused by the mugger, on the one hand; the barely imaginable pain experienced by the child, on the other. Are we to say that your pain is of direct moral relevance, because it is the pain of someone with a sense of justice, but that the child's pain is not of direct moral relevance, because children lack a sense of justice? Are we to say that your minor pain counts for more, from the moral point of view, than does the much greater pain of the child, because your pain is the pain of someone with a sense of justice, the child's not? Are we to say that part of the direct wrong done to you consists of the pain the mugger has caused, but that no direct wrong is done to the child, again because you have a sense of justice, something the unfortunate child lacks?

Rawls commits himself to saying all of this; I do not think there can be any question that this is where his thinking leads him. Neither, then, can there be any question, in my mind at least, that he is guilty of a prejudicial way of thinking about the moral status of children and other human beings lacking in rational capacities. (That he is not alone in this will be shown in chapter 6, both in the discussion of Moral Elitism and in the assessment of Kant's ideas.) In any event, if morality is interpreted in terms of interests, the interests of some human beings cannot be ignored and cannot count for less than the like interests of other human beings simply because some do, while others do not, have a sense of justice.

As for other-than-human animals: they do not fare well, given the Rawlsian perspective. For while the veil of ignorance shields contractors from detailed knowledge of their personal identity, there is one rather important fact they are permitted to know. They all know that they will enter and exit the world as human beings. There can be no surprise, therefore, when Rawls denies that we have direct duties to animals. Rational, self-interested contractors *can-*

not have self-interested reasons for recognizing the direct moral relevance of the interests of animals nor, therefore, any direct duties owed in their case. Why not? Because contractors know that *they* (the human contractors) will never be one of *them* (a nonhuman animal). That Rawls denies direct duties to animals thus is preordained, the outcome in the stacked deck as dealt.

Some critics believe that the part of Rawls's position just summarized suffers from a moral prejudice analogous to racism and sexism. The prejudice is speciesism, understood as assigning greater weight to the interests of human beings, just because they are human interests, compared with the interests of nonhuman animals, just because they are not human interests. Rawls does do this; I do not think there can be any doubt that he does. The important question is whether, in doing so, his views may be correctly and fairly described as prejudicial. I think they can.

A variation on our earlier example will help explain why. A mugger has pushed you to the ground and stolen your money; you are left with a number of cuts and bruises—minor, to be sure, but still painful. Next, let us try to imagine the pain felt by the dogs who were vivisected by the scientists at Port Royal—the dogs who, without the benefit of anesthetic, had their four paws nailed to boards before being slit open. Are we to say that your pain is of direct moral relevance, because it is human pain, but that the dogs' pain is not of direct moral relevance, because it is canine pain? Are we to say that your minor pain counts for more, from the moral point of view, than the much greater pain of the dogs, because your pain is the pain of a human being, the dogs' not? Are we to say that a direct wrong was done to you because of the pain caused by the mugger, but that no direct wrong was done to the dogs, again because your pain is human pain, their pain not?

Rawls commits himself to saying all of this, too; I do not think there can be any question that he does. Neither, then, can there be any question that he is guilty of a prejudicial (if all too common, at least among philosophers) way of thinking about morality. From the point of view of elementary justice, as noted above, the interests of some human beings cannot be ignored and cannot count for less than the like interests of other human beings simply because they do not belong to the "right" race or gender. The same is true when it comes to species membership. From the point of view of elementary justice, the interests of animals cannot be ignored and cannot count for less than the like interests of human beings simply because animals do not belong to the "right" species. And just as it is true that assigning a privileged moral status to some people and, implicitly, assigning a lower status to others, solely on the basis of race or gender, is a classic expression of racism and sexism, so it is true that assigning a privileged moral status to human beings and, implicitly, assigning a lower status to every other animal, solely on the basis of species membership, is a classic expression of an analogous prejudice: speciesism.

SPECIESISM

Rawls never responds to this criticism; the philosopher Carl Cohen does. A self-avowed speciesist ("and proud of it"), Cohen believes that human suffering counts for more than the equal suffering of animals because humans are human. Whereas "there is no morally relevant distinction among human ethnic groups," Cohen maintains that "the morally relevant differences [between humans and other animals] are enormous." In particular, human beings but not other animals are "morally autonomous"; we can, but they cannot, make moral choices for which we are morally responsible.

This defense of speciesism is no defense at all. Not only does it conveniently overlook the fact that a very large percentage of the human population (children for the first several years of their lives, for example) is not morally autonomous, moral autonomy (and the same is true of Rawls's "sense of justice") is not relevant to the issues at hand. An example will help explain why.

Imagine someone says that Jack is smarter than Jill because Jack lives in Syracuse, Jill in San Francisco. Where the two live is different, certainly; and where different people live sometimes is a relevant consideration (for example, when a census is being taken or taxes are levied). But everyone will recognize that where Jack and Jill live has no logical bearing on whether Jack is smarter. To think otherwise is to commit a fallacy of irrelevance familiar to anyone who has taken a course in elementary logic.

The same is no less true when a speciesist says that Toto's suffering counts for less than the equal suffering of Dorothy because Dorothy, but not Toto, is morally autonomous; or because Dorothy, but not Toto, has a sense of justice. If the question we are being asked is whether Jack is smarter than Jill, we are given no relevant reason for thinking one way or the other if we are told that Jack and Jill live in different cities. Similarly, if the question we are being asked is "Does Toto's pain count as much as Dorothy's?" we are given no relevant reason for thinking one way or the other if we are told that Dorothy is morally autonomous, while Toto is not, or that Dorothy, but not Toto, has a sense of justice.

This lack of a relevant reason is not because the capacity for moral autonomy, for example, is never relevant to our moral thinking about the interests of humans and other animals. Sometimes it is. If Jack and Jill have this capacity, they (but not Toto) will have an interest in being free to act as their conscience dictates. In this sense, the difference between Jack and Jill, on the one hand, and Toto, on the other, *is* morally relevant. But just because moral autonomy is morally relevant to the assessment and weighting of *some* interests, it does not follow that it is relevant to the assessment and weighting of *all* interests. And one interest to which it is not relevant is the interest in avoiding pain. Logically, to discount Toto's pain because Toto is not morally autonomous is fully analogous to discounting Jill's intelligence because she does not live in Syracuse.

The question, then, is whether any defensible, relevant reason can be offered in support of the speciesist judgment that the moral importance of the pains of humans and those of animals, equal in other respects (I note that the same applies to equal pleasures, benefits, harms, and interests, for example), always should be weighted in favor of the human being over the animal being? To this question, neither Rawls nor Cohen (nor any other philosopher, for that matter) offers a logically relevant answer. To persist in judging human interests as being more important than the like interests of other animals because they are human interests is not rationally defensible. Speciesism is a moral prejudice. And (contrary to Cohen's assurances to the contrary), it is wrong, not right.

Once we recognize that, save at the cost of moral prejudice, the interests of animals cannot be ignored or discounted *because they are the interests of animals*, the way is cleared for recognizing direct duties in their case. As noted earlier, direct duties are owed to those whose interests are directly morally relevant. Contrary to the Cartesians among us, nonhuman animals *have* interests; and contrary to both simple and Rawlsian contractarians, the interests of animals *are* directly morally relevant. As such, animals who have interests are owed direct duties. This is the conclusion we reach, given the preceding analysis, a conclusion that finds additional corroboration by considering the following.

Suppose I maliciously break your leg, thereby causing you serious injury and a great deal of gratuitous pain. Next, suppose I maliciously break your dog's leg, thereby causing her serious injury and a great deal of gratuitous pain. My two actions are relevantly similar: in each I do something, for no good reason, that causes another individual serious injury and a great deal of pain. Now, relevantly similar cases should be judged similarly. This principle is axiomatic if our moral thinking is to be nonarbitrary and nonprejudicial.

And our moral thinking is neither nonarbitrary nor nonprejudicial in the present case if we think as follows: my maliciously breaking your leg represents my failure to fulfill a duty I have directly to you, because you have an interest in being spared serious injury and gratuitous pain, but my maliciously breaking your dog's leg does not represent a failure to fulfill a duty I have directly to your dog, even though she has a comparable interest in being spared serious injury and gratuitous pain. It is only if we are willing arbitrarily or prejudicially to judge relevantly similar cases differently that we can suppose that the duty in the one case is direct, in the other not. One of this chapter's main purposes has been to show why we should not be willing to do this.

Of course, one could, and as we have seen Cartesians do, deny that nonhuman animals are aware of anything, including pain, a maneuver that would blunt the force of the objection that Rawlsian contractarianism is prejudicial. If animals do not feel anything no matter what we do to them, it would not be prejudicial to affirm that we have a direct duty to avoid causing human beings gratuitous pain, on the one hand, and to deny that we have this same duty directly to animal beings, on the other. To his credit, Rawls is too much in the grip of a robust common sense to believe that the dogs at Port Royal felt nothing and thus did not, because they could not, suffer. Rawls's problem is not that he consorts with today's neo-Cartesians, including those who, like Carruthers, use their Cartesianism as a basis for their contractarianism; his problem is that his moral outlook prejudicially excludes nonhuman animals from direct moral concern.

Indirect duty views, I believe, including the most ingenious among them, and despite their several merits, are and must be unsatisfactory in general, unsatisfactory when it comes to the moral status of animals in particular. In this latter context, those who favor indirect duty views have a choice: *either* they can rest their position on the claim that animals lack interests (the Cartesian option favored by Carruthers) *or* they can rest their position on the claim that, while animals have interests, their interests are of no direct moral concern (the non-Cartesian option favored by Rawls). For reasons given in this chapter, both options are unsatisfactory. Whatever else may be in doubt, this much is clear: those animals we raise for food, trap for fur, and use in research are owed direct duties. Because (by definition) indirect duty views deny direct duties to nonhuman animals, every indirect duty view is, and every indirect duty view must be, mistaken. The following chapter examines two moral theories that, even while they deny that animals have rights against us, affirm that we have direct duties to them.

5

DIRECT DUTY VIEWS

H umans and animals are owed direct duties. This much we know. Can we know more than this? In particular, can we know what duties are owed and why we owe them? This chapter examines two answers to these questions, each of which dispenses with the idea of rights, human rights as well as animal rights. The cruelty-kindness view, which for reasons of simplicity I will sometimes refer to as "cruelty-kindness," is discussed first; this is followed by a discussion of a particular interpretation of the position known as utilitarianism. Both moral theories are examples of direct duty views— theories that, in contrast to all indirect duty views, maintain that nonhuman animals are owed direct duties.

THE CRUELTY-KINDNESS VIEW

Simply stated, the cruelty-kindness view maintains that we have a direct duty to be kind to animals and a direct duty not to be cruel to them. To say that the duty of kindness is direct means that kindness is owed to animals themselves, not to those humans who might be affected by how animals are treated. And the same is true of the prohibition against cruelty: our duty not to be cruel is owed to animals directly.

Some philosophers who favor kindness and condemn cruelty to animals deny that the duty in either case is direct. These philosophers encourage kindness and discourage cruelty to animals because of the effect these behaviors have on human character and what this portends for how humans will be treated. Writes the great Prussian philosopher Immanuel Kant: "Tender feelings toward dumb animals develop humane feelings toward mankind." This is why we should be kind to animals. As for cruelty: "[H]e who is cruel to animals becomes hard also in his dealings with men." That is why we should not be cruel to them.

CHAPTER 5

Kant is not alone in thinking this way. The seventeenth-century English philosopher John Locke shares the same perspective. Locke writes:

One thing I have frequently observed in Children is that when they have got possession of any poor creature they are apt to use it ill. They often torment, and treat very roughly, young Birds, Butterflies, and such other poor Animals, which fall into their Hands, and that with a seeming kind of Pleasure. This I think should be watched in them if they incline to any such Cruelty, they should be taught the contrary Usage. For the Custom of Tormenting and Killing of Beasts, will, by Degrees, harden their Minds even towards Men; and they who delight in the Suffering and Destruction of Inferior Creatures, will not be apt to be very compassionate, or benign to those of their own kind.

Both Kant and Locke are on the side of truth when it comes to human moral development. Recent studies confirm, what people of common sense have long suspected, that a pattern of cruelty to animals in a person's youth is frequently correlated with a pattern of violent behavior toward humans in adult life. This is certainly *a* reason to discourage cruelty to animals. Still, this cannot be the *only* reason, nor can it be the *main* one, if cruelty-kindness is interpreted as a direct duty view. Interpreted in this way, both the duty to be kind and the duty not to be cruel are owed to animals themselves.

The cruelty-kindness view makes an important contribution to our understanding of morality. First, by recognizing that direct duties are owed to non-human animals, cruelty-kindness overcomes the prejudice of speciesism common to both simple and Rawlsian versions of contractarianism. Second, any credible moral outlook arguably should find a place for kindness and against cruelty, not only when it comes to how animals are treated but also when it comes to our treatment of one another.

If fully generalized, cruelty-kindness offers the broad outlines of a distinctive moral theory. Right acts are right because they are acts of kindness, wrong acts are wrong because they are acts of cruelty. Analogous direct duty views might select a different pair of comparable polar moral opposites. For example, an ethic of love would assert that acts are right if they are expressive of love, wrong if they are expressive of hate. Other candidates are compassion and indifference, or reverence for life and malice toward life. Although the focus here is on cruelty-kindness, I believe the logic of my criticisms encompasses these and other relevantly similar theories. All such theories, I believe, confuse assessments of the moral character people display in acting as they do with assessments of the morality of what they do.

52

To understand the cruelty-kindness view obviously presupposes that we understand the two key ideas: cruelty, on the one hand, kindness, on the other. To take up the latter idea first: People express kindness when they act out of concern for or with compassion toward another. Kindness moves us to do things that advance the well-being of others, either by finding ways to satisfy their preference interests (what they are interested in having or doing) or by tending to their welfare interests (what is in their interests). For many of us, perhaps even for all, the best people we know are generous when it comes to kindness, freely giving of their time, effort, and (when possible) money to those in need. The world, we think, would be a much better place if there were more kind people in it.

The vice of cruelty occupies a moral space opposite to that of kindness. People or their acts are cruel if they display either a lack of sympathy for causing another to suffer (what I will call "indifferent cruelty") or positive enjoyment in causing it (referred to as "sadistic cruelty"). Recall the words Locke uses when he describes the cruelty he sometimes finds in children: they "torment" their victims, treat their victims "very roughly," "use [their victims] ill," and do so "with a seeming kind of Pleasure." Some children, Locke is saying, are sadistically cruel. That he limits his comments to children who are cruel to animals should not obscure the fact that the same behaviors define sadistic cruelty to humans. Anytime anyone enjoys making anybody suffer, sadistic cruelty rears its ugly head.

Cruelty-kindness clearly represents an improvement over indirect duty views when it comes to questions regarding moral standing. Who counts morally? For advocates of cruelty-kindness, the answer is, "All those toward whom we can act either cruelly or kindly." Who does not count morally? For advocates of cruelty-kindness, the answer is, "All those toward whom we cannot act either cruelly or kindly." Because we can act in these ways toward rationally competent members of various minority groups, these individuals (unlike the verdict available to simple contractarians) have moral standing, according to cruelty-kindness. And because we can act in these ways toward children who lack a sense of justice, for example, these children (unlike the verdict reached by Rawlsian contractarians) also have moral standing according to cruelty-kindness.

As for other-than-human animals: cruelty-kindness offers a far more welcoming moral outlook than either form of contractarianism. Along with Father Rickaby (his views were mentioned in chapter 1), cruelty-kindness denies that sticks and stones have moral standing; nothing we can do to them can be meaningfully construed as being either kind or cruel. But contrary to the good

Father, advocates of cruelty-kindness make a different judgment in the case of calves on farms and scrub jays in laboratories, for example. Because we can treat these and other mammals or birds cruelly or kindly, they are not "of the order of sticks and stones." Unlike the latter, these animals have moral standing.

Evaluating Cruelty-Kindness

As has been remarked already, too few people have the virtue of kindness. Nevertheless, and notwithstanding its cherished status, the presence of kindness is no guarantee of right action. While being motivated by kindness is a good thing as far as it goes, there is no guarantee that a kind act is the right act. Someone who helps a child abuser find new victims doubtless acts kindly toward the abuser. But none of us will infer that helping the abuser is therefore the right thing to do. The virtue of kindness is one thing; the moral rightness of our actions another.

Cruelty fares no better as a general criterion of moral wrongness. Cruelty in all its guises is a bad thing, a lamentable human failing, something that, while it is not restricted to people who exploit animals, is not unknown in their case. Consider the following passage from Joan Dunayer, describing the behavior of a young researcher:

> In one laboratory, a rat placed on a small cardboard box had his head immobilized by a vice. When a postdoctoral vivisector started drilling into his skull, the rat began to struggle. Held by the head, he attempted to run. His lower body fell over the box's edge. The rat dangled there, struggling. The drilling continued. Some minutes later, the rat kicked over the box, forcing the vivisector to stop and inject him with some anesthetic. Before the anesthetic took effect, the vivisector resumed drilling. Again the rat struggled. Finally, ten minutes into the vivisection, the rat quieted.

Here we have a disturbing case of what appears to be indifferent cruelty: someone who, without empathy or sympathy, chooses to inflict pain even while in possession of the means to prevent it. Next, as an example of sadistic cruelty, consider the behavior Gail Eisnitz documents in her book about the American slaughter industry in general, hog slaughter in particular.

Hog slaughter represents a variation on the main theme of the meatpacking industry. Hogs are driven up a narrow restrainer where the "stunner" gives them an electric shock that is supposed to render them unconscious. They are then shackled with chains attached to their rear legs, hoisted so that they dangle upside down, and placed on a conveyor belt where they meet the "sticker," whose job is to slit the animals' throats. After being bled to death, the pigs are submerged in a tank of boiling water, then eviscerated, having never regained consciousness. At least this is the way things are supposed to work in theory. As a matter of practice, as Eisnitz found after speaking with workers, actual hog slaughter frequently does not measure up to theory.

The following is a not untypical example. Donny Tice and Alec Wainwright (in order to protect her sources, Eisnitz changed their names) are interviewed. In an earlier conversation, Tice had described some of the things he did to the hogs. It was now Wainwright's turn. Writes Eisnitz:

> Not yet out of his teens, Wainright had already been working as a day-shift shackler for two years.
>
> Wainwright talked about the same games as Tice had—the stun operator would intentionally mis-stun hogs so that Wainwright would have a hard time shackling them.
>
> "Sometimes," he said, "when the chain stops for a little while and we have time to screw around with the hog, we'll half stun it. It'll start freakin' out, going crazy. It'll be sitting there yelping."
>
> Other times, when a hog would get loose outside the catch pen, [Wainwright] and his co-workers would chase it up to the scalding tank and force it to jump in. "When that happens," he said, "we tell the foreman he accidentally jumped in."
>
> Wainwright had little new to add to what Tice had already told me, but he did confirm Tice's claims of gratuitous cruelty to the animals. And while Tice's confession had seemed both painful and cathartic for him, Wainwright, in telling me of his atrocities against the already doomed pigs, chortled with delight as if recounting a schoolboy prank.
>
> "Why do you do it?" I asked.
>
> "Because it's something to do," Wainwright said. "Like when our utility guy takes the ol' bar and beats the hell out of the hogs in the catch pen. That's kind of fun. I do it, too."
>
> "How often do you do it?"
>
> "I dunno," he replied.

To "beat the hell" out of an animal and find it "kind of fun" illustrates the depths of cruelty to which we humans can sink. Perhaps Eisnitz is correct when she sees workers like Tice and Wainwright, not just the pigs going to slaughter, as victims of the system of mechanized death that defines day-to-day activities in America's twenty-seven hundred slaughterhouses. But even if this is true, there can be no doubt that indifferent cruelty and sadistic cruelty are not strangers among the men and women who work in the packing industry, nor any doubt that the existence of such cruelty leaves a major moral question unanswered. For just as knowing that an act is kind does not guarantee that it is right, so the presence of cruelty does not guarantee that what is done is wrong. Here is an example from another quarter that illustrates the distinctions at issue.

Most physicians who perform abortions are not cruel people; they are not indifferent to the pain they cause, and neither do they enjoy causing it. Still, it is possible that some physicians bring a warped moral sense to their work; in their case, nothing pleases them more than making those in their care suffer. The existence of cruel abortionists certainly is a possibility. Suppose it is more than that; suppose there actually are such physicians. Even granting that there are, it should be clear that the existence of cruel abortionists would not make abortion wrong, anymore than the existence of kind abortionists would make abortion right. To think otherwise is to confuse moral assessments of what people do (whether what someone does is right or wrong) with assessments of their moral character, their virtues and vices. The two are logically distinct. People can do what is wrong while acting from a good motive (recall the person who as an act of kindness helps the child abuser find new victims) just as people can do what is right from a bad motive. It happens everyday.

The logical distinction between (1) morally assessing people and (2) morally assessing their acts applies as much to cruelty and kindness to animals as it does to cruelty and kindness to humans. Here is an example that illustrates the general point. Suppose some researchers who experiment on cats are more considerate than some of their peers. They try to make the cats comfortable and use analgesics to eliminate their pain. Their peers, by contrast, are cruel; they are largely indifferent to or enjoy the pain they deliberately inflict on the cats. Without a doubt we would think better of the former researchers than we do of the latter. But what we think of them *as people* goes no way toward determining the morality of what they *do*—namely, use cats in research. Whether this is right or wrong depends on the morality of what they do, not on the qualities of character they exhibit in doing it. Even if it were true that none of the animals exploited for food, fashion, and knowledge are treated cruelly, that would not tell us whether exploiting them for these purposes is right or wrong. The existence of kind exploiters of animals does not make exploiting them right, anymore than the existence of cruel abortionists makes abortion wrong. Moral assessments of people are, and they should be kept, distinct from moral assessments of what they do. Cruelty-kindness blurs this distinction. Wherever the truth about moral right and wrong might lie, it will not be found in the cruelty-kindness view.

UTILITARIANISM

Some people think the direct duty view we are looking for is utilitarianism. Like contractarianism, utilitarianism takes different forms, and while it may be an exaggeration to say that there are as many forms of utilitarianism as there are utilitarians, the position does seem to be a breeding ground for internal dissent. Understandably, therefore, what I have to say will be selective. Having duly acknowledged this limitation, it is worth noting that the particular form of utilitarianism I discuss, preference utilitarianism (which, for reasons of simplicity, I sometimes refer to as "utilitarianism"), is the one favored by both R. G. Frey and Peter Singer, the two philosophers who have had the most influence in the area of ethics and animals, approached from a utilitarian perspective.

Preference utilitarians accept two principles. The first is a principle of equality: everyone's preferences count, and similar preferences must be counted as having similar weight or importance. If you are interested in listening to Brahms, that counts. If someone else is interested in listening to Boys 'n' the Hood, that counts, too. And if the preferences in both cases are equal, then their satisfaction or frustration counts the same. The morally prejudicial discrimination that simple contractarianism can justify, where greater weight may be given to the interests of some human beings just because they belong to a favored race or gender, for example, is disallowed by utilitarianism.

The same is true when it comes to discrimination based on species membership. Both simple and Rawlsian contractarianism are hospitable to species- ist ways of thinking. Not utilitarianism. *We owe it to animals themselves* to take their preferences into account and to count their preferences fairly. Similar preferences must be assigned the same weight, the same importance, whether the preferences are those of humans or other animals. Our duty to count their equal interests equally is a direct duty we have to animal beings.

The second principle utilitarians accept (about which I will have more to say below) is that of utility: we ought to do the act that brings about the best overall balance between totaled preference satisfactions and totaled preference frustrations for everyone affected by the outcome.

Preference utilitarians thus give a distinctly different answer to questions about moral right and wrong. Acts are right if they lead to the best overall consequences (the best overall balance between totaled preference satisfactions and totaled preference frustrations) for everyone affected, while acts that result in less than the best overall consequences are more or less wrong, depending on how bad the consequences are. For utilitarians, our acts are like arrows that, when right, hit the moral "bull's eye," and that, when wrong, miss the target by a greater or lesser amount.

Utilitarianism's Strengths

Utilitarianism's egalitarianism clearly represents an improvement over simple and Rawlsian contractarianism when it comes to saying who has moral standing. Who counts morally? For utilitarians, the answer is, "All those who have interests." Who does not count morally? For utilitarians, the answer is, "Whatever does not have interests." Because rationally competent members of various minority groups have interests, these individuals (unlike the verdict available to simple contractarians) have moral standing according to utilitarians. And because children who lack a sense of justice have interests, these children (unlike the verdict reached by Rawlsian contractarians) have moral standing too. *Everyone's* interests count, and equal interests must be counted equally, no matter whose interests they are.

In addition, utilitarianism represents an important advance over cruelty-kindness. This latter view, as we have seen, assumes that the morality of what people do is tied to the character traits they exhibit in doing it. This is not true, and utilitarians have an explanation of why it is not. From their perspective, acts are right or wrong depending on their consequences (their results, their effects). Clearly, *why* people act as they do is not one of the consequences, results, or effects of *what* they do. If the kind helper in the earlier discussion of cruelty-kindness is successful, the child abuser will have new children to torment; having these children available will be among the consequences, results, or effects of what is done. That the abuser's helper was motivated by kindness is in a different category altogether. For utilitarians, the character traits people express in acting as they do add nothing to the moral assessment of what they do. On this important matter, utilitarianism proves to be more credible than cruelty-kindness.

Utilitarian Values

Two other important features of preference utilitarianism require further comment. The first concerns what has morally relevant value; the second, what "best overall consequences" means. Regarding the question of value first: preference utilitarians believe that morally relevant positive value resides in the satisfaction of an individual's preferences, while morally relevant negative value is found when an individual's preferences are frustrated. In both cases—that is, both in the case of what has positive value, and in the case of what has negative value—it is the satisfaction or frustration of what individuals are interested in, what they want to do or have, that matters morally, not the individual whose preferences they are. A universe in which you satisfy your desires for water, food, and warmth is, other things being equal, morally better than a universe in which these desires are frustrated. And the same is true in the case of an animal with similar desires. But neither you nor the animal has any morally significant value in your own right.

Here is an analogy to help make the philosophical point clearer. Imagine that some cups contain different liquids, some sweet, some bitter, some a mix of the two. What has value are the liquids: the sweeter, the better; the bitterer, the worse. The cups have no value. It is what goes into them, not what they go into, that has value. For the utilitarian, human beings are like the cups in our example. We have no morally significant value as the individuals we are and thus no equal value. What has morally significant value is what "goes into us," so to speak, the mental states for which we serve as "receptacles." Our feelings of satisfaction have positive value; our feelings of frustration, negative value.

It is also important to be clear about what utilitarians mean by "best overall consequences." This does not mean the best consequences for me alone, or for my family and friends, or for any other person or group taken individually. Instead, to make a fully informed judgment about the best overall consequences, a threefold procedure should be followed. First, we need to identify the satisfactions and frustrations of everyone who will be affected by the choices we might make (for example, by placing the satisfactions in one column, the frustrations in another). Second, we must total all the satisfactions and frustrations for each of the possible actions we are considering. Third, we must determine which act will bring about the best overall balance of totaled satisfactions compared to totaled frustrations. After we have satisfied these procedural requirements, but not before, we are in a position to reach a fully informed moral conclusion. Whatever choice leads to the best overall consequences is where our moral duty lies, and this choice (the one that will bring about the best overall results) will not necessarily lead to the best results for me personally, or for my family, my friends, or a calf raised in close confinement. The best *overall* consequences for everyone concerned are not necessarily the best for each concerned individual.

Evaluating Preference Utilitarianism

I believe preference utilitarianism, despite its appealing features, is not a satisfactory moral theory. The position, as I understand it, is seriously flawed, both procedurally and substantively. Procedurally, it is flawed because it requires that we count the satisfaction of the worst sorts of preferences (what I will call "evil preferences") in reaching a fully informed judgment of moral right or wrong; substantively, it is flawed because, after the necessary calculations have been completed, the worst sorts of acts (what I will call "evil outcomes") can be justified. Later in this chapter, and again in chapter 6, I offer my own account of these two kinds of evil. In the present context, I assume that people of good will who are not already committed to utilitarianism will recognize what I mean by these ideas and will agree with the specific judgments I make. I begin with an example of evil preferences.

In 1989 the national media followed a tragic story involving a group of teenage boys who lured a mentally disadvantaged girl into a basement. Using a broom handle and a baseball bat, four of the boys took turns raping her. What the boys wanted was not sex in the abstract; what they wanted was violent sex forced upon a trusting, uncomprehending girl. (With an IQ of 49, the victim had the mental competence of a second grader).

Preference utilitarians will want to assure us that their moral theory has the wherewithal to explain why what the boys did was wrong. In addition to the terrible things done to the victim, a fully informed moral judgment will have to consider the bad consequences for others, including the anxiety and fear experienced both by the parents in the neighborhood and the other young girls who lived there. Let us assume, for the sake of argument, that utilitarians are able to cite enough bad consequences to support their judgment of wrongdoing. This certainly is the right result. Utilitarianism's first problem concerns the procedure used to get there. That procedure requires that *everyone's* satisfactions and frustrations be taken into account and counted fairly. The poor victim's suffering? Yes. The anxiety of the neighborhood's parents? Yes. Their daughter's fears? Yes. The satisfaction of the rapists' preferences? Yes, indeed. Not to take *their* satisfactions into account would be to treat them unfairly.

How otherwise sensible, sensitive people, people whose philosophical abilities I admire and whose character I respect, can subscribe to a view with this implication always has been, is now, and always will remain a mystery to me.

Are we to count the satisfactions of child abusers before condemning child abuse? Those of slaveholders before denouncing slavery? The very idea of guaranteeing a place for these satisfactions in the "moral calculus" is morally offensive. The preference satisfactions of those who act in these ways should play no role whatsoever in the determination of the wrong they do. We are not to evaluate the violation of human dignity by first asking how much the violators enjoy violating it. That is part of what it means to judge the preferences evil.

For its part, preference utilitarianism is unable to deny a rightful place for such preferences, if our judgment is to be fully informed. Consistent preference utilitarians cannot say, "What the boys did was wrong, which is why we do not have to count their satisfactions." Consistent utilitarians cannot say this because, from their perspective, a fully informed moral judgment of wrongdoing cannot be made before the necessary calculations have been carried out, and the necessary calculations cannot be carried out without including the preference satisfactions of the rapists. Consistency is a virtue, certainly. But consistency is no guarantee of truth. Any credible position concerning the nature of morality should be able to explain why some preference satisfactions simply do not count in the determination of moral right and wrong. Because utilitarians who are consistent will count the rapists' satisfactions in reaching a fully informed judgment concerning the morality of what the boys did, we have reason enough, I believe, to look for a better way to understand what makes right acts right, wrong acts wrong.

The logic of this line of criticism includes more than the preference satisfactions of the direct agents of wrongdoing. By all accounts, other boys in the neighborhood wanted to watch the rape and derived satisfaction from doing so; that being so, the procedure favored by utilitarians obliges us to count their satisfactions, too, before reaching a fully informed moral judgment about the morality of what took place. This cannot be right. If the satisfactions of the rapists should play no role in the determination of the morality of their actions, the same is no less true of the satisfactions of those who supported and approved of their wrongdoing; the satisfaction of their preferences do not count either.

In addition to its flawed procedure, preference utilitarianism also can be faulted for the conclusions it reaches. The worst sorts of acts not only can be permitted, they can emerge as positively obligatory, judged by utilitarian standards. The murder of the innocent illustrates the general problem. All that is necessary to justify this evil is that the best overall consequences obtain, something that can happen in the real world, not just in futuristic works of science fiction. The elderly and the seriously disabled of all ages, for example, often are a burden to their families and society in general. It is, I think, undeniably true that better *overall* consequences would result, in some of these cases, if some of these people had their lives "humanely" terminated. Would we be doing anything wrong if we participated in killing such a person, someone innocent of any serious moral or legal crime, someone not facing imminent death, someone who wants to go on living? Not according to consistent preference utilitarianism. To kill the innocent in such cases, to murder them, not only is not wrong—if we assume their murder brings about the best overall consequences, murdering the innocent is morally obligatory. Few, if any, utilitarians will welcome this result.

In response to this line of criticism, some preference utilitarians (Singer is one of the principal architects of this way of thinking) note that, unlike flowers or snails, the victims in our example have preferences about the future; in particular, they prefer to go on living. To end their lives, to murder them, means that this latter preference will never be satisfied. Even if we arranged to bring a new human being into existence, one whose life prospects were generally better than the quality of life the victims experienced, that, it may be argued, would not change two important facts: (1) if someone is murdered, then that person's preference to go on living will never be satisfied; and (2) the newly conceived "replacement," given the total absence of mind in the case of the human embryo, cannot prefer to go on living. In this sense, and for these reasons, individuals who want to go on living are not "replaceable."

Suppose this is true. What difference does it make, what difference can it make, to a preference utilitarian? If we are told that murdering an irreplaceable individual is always wrong no matter what the consequences, we no longer have a consistent utilitarianism. If utilitarianism means anything, it means this: Whether *any* act is right or wrong *always* depends on the consequences for all those affected by the outcome, something that cannot change just in case someone is "irreplaceable."

A consistent preference utilitarian, therefore, must recognize that the morality of murdering the innocent depends on the consequences, all things considered. So let me again describe the sort of case we are considering. Before us we have someone who is a burden to family and society; someone who is not going to die soon; someone who prefers to go on living. Let us concede the existence of this important preference. Nevertheless, this is all the desire to go on living is: a preference, one that, like every other preference, must be included in the utilitarian calculus, and one that, as is true of every other preference, can be outweighed by aggregating the preference satisfactions of others. To express the same point using different words: a consistent utilitarian must acknowledge that the desire to go on living cannot have the status of a trump that cannot be outweighed by the preferences other people have. Given the complexities of life, there is no reason to deny, and abundant reason to affirm, that, *in some cases*, other people would be better off if steps were taken to end the life of someone who prefers to go on living.

From the perspective of a consistent preference utilitarianism, therefore, murdering the innocent not only is not always wrong—if the consequences for all concerned are "the best," murdering them is morally obligatory. It should not be surprising, therefore, that people with disabilities, who sometimes are a burden to family and society, have publicly expressed fears about their safety, should the day come when the public embraces a utilitarian moral outlook. In my opinion, their fears are entirely justified. A moral theory that subscribes to the principle that the end justifies the means potentially places everyone's life in jeopardy, the lives of the least powerful in particular.

The moral logic of the preceding criticism of utilitarianism is not limited only to the murder of the innocent. On the contrary, this same kind of criticism can be repeated, in all sorts of cases, illustrating time after time how the preference utilitarian's position leads to results that impartial people of good will, people who are not already committed to utilitarianism, will find morally wrong. Lying, cheating, stealing, failing to carry out a solemn promise, arranging to imprison or execute people who are known to be innocent of any crime: all these and countless other acts emerge as right, even obligatory, if the satisfactions for others outweigh the frustrations of the victims. Judged purely in terms of the evil outcomes it can permit or require, preference utilitarianism, even acknowledging its strengths when compared to the other moral positions reviewed in the preceding pages, is not an adequate moral theory.

Utilitarianism and the Treatment of Animals

Utilitarianism's implications concerning how we should treat other animals, as is true of everything else, depends on the overall consequences, counting equal interests equally. This approach can lead to some surprising results. Take sex with animals, for example. Singer comes down on the side of those who want to put this "taboo" (this is his word) in the dustbin of history. Granted, sex involving cruelty to animals is wrong. But, Singer notes, "sex with animals does not always involve cruelty." In fact, when done "in private," "mutually satisfying [sexual] activities [involving animals and humans] may develop." In these cases, consistent with his utilitarian philosophy, Singer finds nothing wrong. One would have hoped that he had. (I address this issue near the end of chapter 7.)

It should be noted, before turning to other matters, that more than bestiality emerges as in principle permissible, given the tenets of preference utilitarianism. Why not lift the "taboo" against having sex with children? After all, it is open to the utilitarian to argue that sex with children need not always involve cruelty. In fact, if done "in private," the utilitarian certainly is free to urge that "mutually satisfying [sexual] activities [involving children and adults] may develop." In these cases, consistent with their philosophy, utilitarians could find nothing wrong. As I explain in the next chapter, the position I favor renders the opposite judgment.

When it comes to other questions concerning the treatment of animals, the utilitarian road becomes no less objectionable. Our ability to know what is right and wrong depends on our ability to know all the relevant consequences, something about which informed, fair-minded people can disagree. A cursory look at commercial animal agriculture illustrates the general point.

In the case of raising and slaughtering animals for food, relevant consequences include how these animals are treated, certainly. Also relevant are the effects of a meat-based diet on human morbidity and mortality; the environmental impact, both of factory farming itself and the crop production required to feed animals raised in close confinement; the interests of distant strangers, people who live in the poorer nations of the world and who succumb to, or live on the edge of, the ravages of famine, and who might conceivably be fed if better-off people ate little or no meat; and the interests of future generations, assuming that not yet existing humans and not yet existing animals have interests.

From a utilitarian perspective, however, fairness requires that we consider much more. For example, the number of Americans whose lives are directly or indirectly linked to current forms of animal agriculture is hardly inconsiderable. Figures provided in the 2001 edition of *Statistical Abstract of the United States* place the number of those who operate and manage animal agricultural operations, along with those who work at such operations or hold jobs directly related to the meat industry, at over 4.5 million. Total farm income from animal production, including dairy and eggs, for that same period, is listed as $192 billion, while the U.S. Department of Agriculture gives the figure $39 billion as the amount of taxes paid by farms of all types in 1996, the most recent year for which tax estimates are available at the time this is written. Add to these figures the millions of other people whose livelihood is indirectly tied to farmed animal production, from truckers to young people flipping burgers at the neighborhood McDonalds; plus the billions of dollars of income and taxes generated as a result of these arrangements; plus the many millions of those who are the dependents of employees whose economic situation is directly or indirectly related to animal agriculture production; plus the dietary tastes and preferences of the (roughly) 98 percent of Americans who like eating meat and spend their money accordingly—add all this together (if one could) and we begin to glimpse both the magnitude of the massive impact animal agriculture has on the United States economy and the costs, financial as well as personal, of abolishing commercial animal agriculture as we know it.

With such large numbers, representing far from trivial human interests, there is little wonder that different people can reach different conclusions about whether raising animals for human consumption is wrong, judged from a utilitarian perspective. Singer, a utilitarian, thinks it is. Frey, another utilitarian, disagrees. But with all due respect to the sincerity of their professed beliefs, it has to be said that neither has provided the kind of detailed analysis their theory requires. What are the benefits? What are the costs? For whom? When? Where? How? When we read Frey and Singer (and I encourage everyone to do so), the data they are obliged to present before rendering an informed judgment is conspicuous for its absence. It is as if each knows which judgment utilitarian calculation favors without having to do the hard work both would impose on the rest of us.

Of course, if it was possible for utilitarians to deny the moral relevance of human preferences and to focus exclusively on how farmed animals are treated, the utilitarian case against contemporary animal agriculture would be clear-cut. The aggregate of the harms done to the billions of animals raised and slaughtered annually in the United States is vast given any reasonable estimate. But a consistent preference utilitarianism cannot do this; by its very nature, it cannot exclude relevant human interests, including those of farmers, their families, and the majority of American consumers. Which illustrates why utilitarianism will always be biased in favor of defending the status quo. In the nature of the case, *the theory must always count the preferences of the majority of people* (often, as in the case of meat eaters, roughly 98% of Americans) who like things just the way they are. If one is looking for a moral theory with which to forge radical social change, utilitarianism looks to be a very poor choice. (I will have more to say on this matter in chapter 6.) In any event, before the preference utilitarian can render a fully informed moral evaluation of animal agriculture, *all* the relevant interests must be taken into account and evaluated fairly.

Let us suppose that somebody somehow is able to carry out all the necessary calculations. Three possibilities present themselves. (1) The current system of animal agriculture leads to better overall consequences than any alternative. (2) The current system leads to worse overall consequences than other alternatives. (3) The current system leads to overall consequences that are equal to those that would flow from other alternatives. If the first option were shown to be true, nothing would follow regarding the moral acceptability of the current system; if the second, nothing would follow concerning the moral acceptability of the current system; and the same is true of the third alternative. In short, *whatever* the overall consequences happen to be, the central moral question, "Is the current system morally acceptable?" will remain unanswered. And it will remain unanswered because (a) consistent utilitarians must count evil preferences just as much as other preferences (all preferences count, and equal preferences must be counted equally) and because (b) their theory, consistently applied, sanctions evil outcomes as much as it sanctions other outcomes.

Whether our questions concern the morality of how humans *or* animals are treated, therefore, we do well to look for answers outside utilitarian theory. The next chapter offers a fresh start, one that, I believe, leads to a more satisfactory moral theory than those considered up to now.

6

HUMAN RIGHTS

The previous two chapters examined a number of influential moral theories; while each contains something of enduring importance, all are arguably deficient in fundamental respects. Is it possible to fashion a way to think about morality that has none of their weaknesses and all of their strengths? If so, where might one begin? And what might such a theory look like?

RECONCEPTUALIZING VALUES

The place to begin, I think, is with the utilitarian's view of the value of the individual—or, rather, lack of value. That individuals lack morally significant value is a central tenet of utilitarianism, something that was illustrated in the previous chapter by means of the analogy of cups and their contents. It is not the cups themselves (not the individuals we are) that have morally significant value; rather, it is what the cups contain (the quality of our experience, the satisfaction or frustration of our interests) that have such value.

Suppose we conceptualize the matter differently. Instead of thinking that *the interests individuals have* are what has fundamental moral value, we think that it is *the individuals who have interests* who have such value. To think about morality in this way is Kantian in spirit, though, as we shall see below, not Kantian in letter. Kant gives the name *worth* to the kind of value under discussion; I prefer *inherent value*, *inherent* because the kind of value in question belongs to those individuals who have it (it is not something conferred on them as the result of a contract, for example), and *value* because what is designated is not some merely factual feature shared by these individuals but is instead what makes them morally equal. To say that individuals are inherently valuable is to say that they are something more than, and in fact something different from, mere receptacles of valued mental states. In our case, it is the persons we are, not the positive or negative feelings we experience, who have fundamental moral value. To refer to our working analogy, it is the cups, not the liquids they contain, that have such value.

In his philosophy, Kant interprets worth in terms of what he calls "end in itself." Kant is not denying that we can be useful as a means to one another, as when a plumber fixes a leaky faucet or a dentist fills a tooth; instead, he is affirming that it is wrong to treat one another *merely* as means. The theory I favor concurs. Whenever we take informed choice away from persons, or coercively impose our will on them, in pursuit of some selfish or social good, what we do is morally wrong. We reduce the moral worth (the inherent value) of persons to what is of instrumental value only. We treat people as if they were things.

The recognition of inherent value gives us a theoretical leg to stand on, so to speak, as we begin to fashion a distinctively different moral theory. Central to the theory I favor is the duty of respect, by which I mean the following: Those individuals who possess inherent value are owed the direct duty of respectful treatment. The reverse is true as well. Those individuals who are owed the direct duty of respect possess inherent value. As for the duty of respect, the requirement is simple and, again, Kantian in spirit. Individuals who have inherent value are never to be treated as if they were of instrumental value only. Whenever this occurs, whenever they are treated "merely as means," as if they had the value of things, these individuals are treated with a lack of respect.

What makes right acts right? What makes wrong acts wrong? My initial answers to the central questions of moral theory are simple: Acts are right when inherently valuable individuals are treated with respect, wrong when they are treated with a lack of respect. An example should make my meaning clearer.

THE TUSKEGEE SYPHILIS STUDY

The time: 1932. The place: Tuskegee Institute (now Tuskegee University), in Tuskegee, Alabama, among the nation's oldest, most respected African American institutions of higher learning. The study's sponsor: the U.S. Public Health Service. The participants: 399 impoverished African American men who volunteered to receive, without charge, what they were told was "special treatment" for their "bad blood," not knowing that in fact they suffered from syphilis and that the "medicine" they were given was not medicine at all and would have no therapeutic effect.

Also unknown to the participants was the reason for the study. It was not to help them recover from their illness; it was not even to find a cure for syphilis; instead, the study was conducted to determine what would happen to the men if their condition went untreated. To learn this, the researchers thought, would help physicians understand the long-term effects of syphilis. Armed with this knowledge, syphilis sufferers in the future could receive better treatment.

Remarkably, in a country founded on respect for human dignity, the study was carried out on these uninformed, trusting men, from 1932 to 1972—for *forty* years—with funds from, and with the knowing support of, the United States government.

All this is bad enough. What makes matters worse is that even after it became known, in 1957, that syphilis could be treated successfully using penicillin, the researchers withheld the cure. The results? By the time the true purpose of the study was exposed, twenty-eight men had died from the disease, another one hundred had died from related complications, forty wives had been infected, and nineteen children had been born with syphilis.

Now, utilitarians, we know, will canvass all these bad consequences, as their procedure requires, before rendering their judgment. This is decidedly not the way to proceed, given the view I favor. These tragic consequences are lamentable, certainly. They make a bad thing worse. But they are not the grounds of the fundamental wrong. They are consequences of the fundamental wrong: the men in the study were treated merely as means in pursuit of what the researchers hoped would be a good result. As such, they were treated with a lack of respect.

THE DUTY OF RESPECT

It is one thing to describe (even incompletely) a moral theory; it is quite another thing to offer reasons why anyone should accept it. What reasons can be given in the present case? And how compelling are they?

The best place to begin is with the duty of respect. Why think we have this duty? The grounds for recognizing the duty to treat one another with respect grow out of the objections raised against the moral theories discussed in the previous two chapters. As we have seen, simple contractarianism (Rawls's treatment of contractarianism is taken up near the end of this chapter) makes a valuable contribution when it emphasizes the importance of reason in determining what is morally right and wrong; but this same position can be faulted because it permits those who frame the moral contract prejudicially to exploit others (those the contractors have self-interested reasons to exclude), the members of racial minorities being among the obvious candidates. Any adequate moral theory should prohibit such prejudicial exclusion. The theory I favor satisfies this requirement. For reasons that will become clearer as we proceed (see the discussion of moral elitism, below), the duty of respect is owed to all persons regardless of considerations relating to race, gender, sexual orientation, and age, for example.

Any adequate moral theory must be able to distinguish between moral assessments of what people do, on the one hand, and moral assessments of the character they display in doing it, on the other. As has been argued, cruelty-kindness is unable to do this. By contrast, the theory I favor satisfies this requirement. Recall the teenage rapists. Imagine they all were sadistically cruel, each taking intense pleasure in abusing their victim; or imagine they all were coolly indifferent to the pain and fear they caused. In either case, we could not help but look upon these boys as lacking in those feelings that help define the minimal moral expectations of being human. Even so, the cruelty exhibited in such behavior is and must be kept distinct from the moral wrong done. Having a cruel character would help explain why the boys did the wrong they did; it would not explain why what they did was wrong. The theory I favor, by contrast, offers a clear explanation of the wrong done: what the rapists did was wrong because they treated their victim with a lack of respect, treating her as a mere thing, valuable only because she satisfied their desires.

Utilitarianism arguably overcomes the weaknesses of both simple contractarianism and cruelty-kindness while preserving the strengths of each. As is true of simple contractarianism, utilitarianism assigns reason a key role in determining moral right and wrong. In addition, the kinds of prejudice that simple contractarianism can permit, ranging from racism to speciesism, arguably are disallowed by utilitarianism's insistence on counting equal interests equally; and whereas cruelty-kindness is unable clearly to distinguish between moral assessments of what people do and moral assessments of the character they display in doing it, utilitarianism satisfies this requirement, too. With so many important strengths to its credit, utilitarianism is an appealing moral outlook.

However, all things considered, I think we can do better. While the differences between the theory I favor and utilitarianism are many, highlighting two will be enough for present purposes. As we have seen, consistent utilitarians are logically committed to counting the satisfaction of any and every preference; only after we have done this can we make a fully informed judgment about what is right and wrong. This is why the preference satisfactions of the rapists count just as much as the comparably important preference satisfactions of anyone else, including those of their victim.

An adequate moral theory should be able to explain why preferences like those of the rapists are beyond the moral pale. Once again, the theory I favor satisfies this requirement. The preferences of the rapists, let alone their satisfaction, play no role whatsoever in the moral assessment of what they did. From the moral point of view, the question is not "What desires did the boys satisfy by treating their victim as they did?" but "How did they treat her?" *How* they treated her is straightforward: They treated her with a lack of respect, as if she were a thing; fundamentally, this is why what they did was the grievous wrong it was, something that is true, and something we can know to be true, independently of knowing what the rapists wanted. Thus, one way to characterize what evil preferences are, is the following: Evil preferences are those preferences that, when acted upon, lead people to treat inherently valuable individuals as if they were things, having instrumental value only. (I add to this analysis of evil preferences at the end of this chapter.)

Second, as an earlier criticism of utilitarianism attempted to show, this theory permits harming innocent individuals in the name of producing benefits for others. An adequate moral outlook should prohibit exploiting the innocent in this fashion. The theory I favor does. To murder the innocent for this reason, for example, however painlessly, is to treat those who possess inherent value as if they were of instrumental value only—as if their moral status was the same as a pencil or skillet, a pair of roller blades or a Walkman. Whatever language we use, the murder of the innocent is wrong because it wrongs the victim, regardless of the consequences for others.

To conclude this defense of the duty of respect, recall the question asked at the beginning of this chapter: Is it possible to craft a moral theory that has none of the weaknesses and all of the strengths found in the positions examined in the previous two chapters? I believe it is. For the reasons just given, the theory that recognizes the duty of respect owed directly to those individuals who are inherently valuable avoids these weaknesses and preserves these strengths. In the absence of compelling arguments to the contrary, I shall assume that the duty of respect is a valid principle of direct duty, one that is owed to all those human beings who are inherently valuable. Which humans these are remains to be determined.

MORAL ELITISM

As is evident from the preceding, the moral theory I favor involves two central ideas. The first is the inherent value of individuals, understood as a kind of value that is categorically distinct from whatever is merely instrumentally valuable. The second is the duty to treat others with respect, a duty that is honored whenever individuals who are inherently valuable are treated in ways that do not reduce their value to (in Kant's words) "mere means."

To agree that some humans have inherent value leaves open the question whether this is true of all, most, or only a select few among us. Some philosophers favor this last option. This certainly seems to be what Aristotle (384–322 BCE) thinks. He believes that those who possess advanced rational capacities enjoy a more exalted moral status than those who lack them. This has serious implications for those found lacking in this regard. Using this basis, Aristotle classifies women as less morally worthy than men and argues that humans who are deficient when it comes to rational capabilities are born to be the slaves of those who are gifted in their rational endowments.

Aristotle does not err when he identifies reason as an important human capacity; his problems arise because of the inferences he makes after having done so. While moral elitism of the Aristotelian variety may have been an attractive view among members of the educated male aristocracy that flourished in Athens during the fourth century BCE, it will attract few adherents today. Women are not deserving of less moral respect than men, and human beings who do not possess advanced rational abilities are not properly consigned to being the slaves of those who do. If we cannot agree on this, it is difficult to imagine any substantive moral truths on which we can agree.

There is a way to avoid moral elitism's unacceptable implications. This is to recognize that all those who are owed the direct duty of respectful treatment are morally equal, the one to the other, *regardless* of their intellectual brilliance, gender, race, class, age, religion, birthplace, talent, disabilities, and social contribution, for example. The genius and the seriously mentally disadvantaged child; the prince and the pauper; the brain surgeon and the fruit vendor; Mother Teresa and the most unscrupulous used-car salesman: all are owed the direct duty to be treated with respect; all are equally inherently valuable; none are ever to be treated in ways that reduce them to the status of things, as if they existed merely as means to forward the individual or collective interests of others, including some self-proclaimed group of the "moral elite."

MORAL RIGHTS

How do rights enter the picture? As already noted, whether humans (let alone animals) have rights is among moral philosophy's most contentious questions. Any proffered answer, including the one I favor, faces serious challenges. Nevertheless, I believe that recognition of individual moral rights is absolutely essential to an adequate moral theory. My reasons for thinking so are as follows.

Earlier in this chapter I explained why the duty of respect is a valid principle of direct duty, a duty owed to all those who are inherently valuable. In saying it is a valid principle of direct duty, I mean it has the best reasons, the best arguments on its side. If this much is granted, how rights arise can be explained as follows.

In chapter 3, rights were characterized as valid claims. To say they are claims means that rights represent treatment one is justified in demanding, treatment that is strictly owed; to say that such a claim is valid means that the claim is rationally justified. Now, whether a claim to a right is valid depends on whether the basis of the claim is justified. And the basis of such a claim is justified if the basis is a valid principle of direct duty. Thus, if, as has been argued, the obligation to treat one another with respect is a valid principle of direct duty; and if, as was just explained, the validity of a claim depends on the validity of the moral principle on which it rests; then it follows that we have a valid claim to be treated with respect. And since (as we have been assuming throughout) rights are valid claims, it follows that we have a right to be treated with respect. Or (to express these same ideas differently) being treated respectfully is something we are morally entitled to claim as our due, something we are morally justified in requiring of others. Because individual rights occupy a central place in the moral theory I favor, and for reasons of linguistic economy, I sometimes refer to my position as the "rights view."

The right to be treated with respect encapsulates the defining features of moral rights explained in chapter 3. (I will have more to say about these features in the next section.)

- No trespassing: Those who possess this right are protected by an invisible No Trespassing sign. For example, others do not have unrestricted liberty to injure the bodies or deny the freedom of those who have this right.
- Trump: The right to be treated with respect has the status of a trump.

Those individuals who have this right have a valid claim against being treated as mere means in pursuit of some good, whether private or public, chosen by others.

- Equality: The right belongs equally to all those to whom the duty of respectful treatment is owed, regardless of their race or gender, their class or ethnicity, for example.
- Justice: Possession of the right demands justice. Respectful treatment is owed, not something it would be "awfully nice" to receive.

Does the preceding constitute a strict proof of the rights view? I would be the first to say that it does not. In fact, the very idea of a "strict proof," analogous to the kind of proof we find in geometry, for example, is out of place in the context of assessing competing moral theories. What can be done, and what I have attempted to do, is to explain why the rights view has strengths that the other influential theories examined lack; how, unlike the latter, it satisfies a family of reasonable requirements for assessing competing moral theories; and why, therefore, it offers a way to think about morality that is principled, nonarbitrary, nonprejudicial, and rationally defensible. Short of constructing a strict proof, my argument functions to shift the burden of appropriate proof to those who favor some other view, meaning: it will be the burden of others, who disagree with the rights view, to explain where and why it goes wrong, or how some other moral theory has better reasons, stronger arguments on its side. To advance the critical assessment of competing moral theories this far, given the nature of the present volume, it seems to me, may be the best one can hope to do.

WHAT RIGHTS DO HUMANS HAVE?

In chapter three, when the topic of rights was broached for the first time, distinctions were made between (1) legal and moral rights, and (2) positive moral rights and negative moral rights. I indicated there that the argument and analysis contained in these pages would mainly be concerned with negative moral rights, understood as rights not to be harmed or interfered with, whether or not these rights are recognized and protected by the common law. Something more can now be said about positive and negative moral rights.

The moral right to be treated with respect, which is fundamental to the rights view, can be interpreted both as a positive and a negative right. Interpreted as a positive right, possession of this right would impose duties of assistance on others (for example, duties to make educational, health, and other human services available to all). Whether this right has this status is among the most divisive issues in moral and political philosophy, one that, given the nature of the present volume, need not be addressed. For while the possible status of this right as a positive right is disputed by many human rights' advocates, to the best of my knowledge none of these advocates denies that the right to be treated with respect has the status of a negative moral right. This is how I have been interpreting this fundamental human right in the preceding pages, and this is how I will continue to interpret it in what follows.

Now, negative moral rights, we know, have several noteworthy features, including their status as invisible No Trespassing signs and their function as trump. For reasons already given, the fundamental right to be treated with respect shares both of these features. The same is true of the more specific rights mentioned in chapter 3: the rights to life, bodily integrity, and freedom. These three rights correspond to the most important ways in which our value as the persons we are can be assaulted. Those who assume unjustified freedom for themselves may wrongfully deprive us of our lives, invade or injure our bodies, or deny or diminish our freedom, all in the name of some "greater good," whether personal or public. The enumeration of these additional rights thus serves to remind us of more specific aspects of our individuality that are protected (at least they should be) because we share the right to respectful treatment. The No Trespassing and trump functions of moral rights shield our lives, our bodies, and our freedom against the excessive freedom of others. To act in ways that are respectful of individual rights is to act in ways that are respectful of the individuals whose rights they are.

Moreover, each of these more specific rights, as is true of the right to be treated with respect, is possessed equally by those who possess these rights, and the claims made when these rights are invoked are calls for justice not requests for kindness or generosity. Respect for our lives, our bodily integrity, or our freedom is something we are owed, something we are due, as a matter of moral justice.

Does the recognition of these individual rights mean that it is always wrong to embark upon or sustain social practices or institutions that seek to advance the good of society? Again, this is among the most divisive issues in contemporary moral and political theory, one that is intimately connected to asking whether the right to be treated with respect has the status of a positive right. As noted earlier, these matters are not addressed on this occasion. Here, it is enough to remark that, from the perspective of the rights view, whatever benefits some might derive from various policies and institutions, these policies and institutions are wrong if they violate the rights of some in order to secure benefits for others. In this sense, the rights view gives priority to the right to be treated with respect, interpreted as a negative moral right, even if this same right also happens to have the status of a positive moral right.

A final point needs to be clarified before concluding this section. Because so much emphasis is being placed on respectful treatment, an interpreter of the rights view might infer that the pain people suffer at the hands of their abusers does not matter morally. This is not true. The suffering of those who are treated immorally matters, sometimes (as in the case of the poor child who died at the hands of Captain Marshall, for example) profoundly. Even so, it is important to understand why, according to the rights view, and according to Kant's view as well, causing others to suffer is not the fundamental moral wrong. Some examples will help clarify this important point.

People are murdered in a variety of ways. Some victims meet their end only after prolonged torture; others are murdered without having suffered at all. For example, a drink might be laced with an undetectable lethal drug; then, without knowing what has happened, the victim dies painlessly, never having regained consciousness. If the wrongness of murder depended on how much the victim suffered, we would be obliged to say that painless murders are not wrong. But this is absurd. How, then, can we account for why the murder of the innocent is wrong even when the victims do not suffer? And how can this account be extended to cases where those who are murdered suffer a great deal?

The rights view answers these questions as follows. In cases where innocent people are murdered painlessly, their right to be treated with respect is violated; this is what makes their murder wrong. In cases where the victims suffer greatly, the fundamental wrong is the same: a lack of respect, only in these cases the wrong done is compounded by how much the victims suffer. The suffering and other harms people are made to endure at the hands of those who violate their rights is a lamentable, sometimes an unspeakably, tragic feature of the world. Still, according to the rights view, this suffering and these other harms occur *as a consequence* of treating individuals with a lack of respect; as such, as bad as they are, and as much as we would wish them away, the suffering and other harms are not themselves the fundamental wrong.

PERSONS

The rights view, I believe, is rationally the most satisfactory way to think about human morality. The claim we make to respectful treatment is a valid claim, grounded in a valid principle of direct duty. All of us are directly owed treatment that respects our equal inherent value, and each of us possesses an equal right to be treated respectfully. To adopt the rights view, I believe, is to embrace a moral theory that more adequately illuminates and explains the foundations of our duties to one another than the other outlooks we have considered. On this score, the rights view has the best reasons, the best arguments, on its side. One important question that remains to be addressed concerns which humans have rights, assuming that some do.

In his philosophy Kant limits inherent value, or worth, to those humans who are persons. Persons are individuals who possess a variety of sophisticated capacities, reason and autonomy in particular. Because persons are rational, they are able critically to assess the choices they make before making them; because they are autonomous, persons are free to make the choices they do; and because they are both rational and autonomous, persons are morally responsible for what they do and fail to do. For Kant, then, there is an elegant reciprocity in how moral responsibility and moral rights are related. All, and only those, who are morally responsible have moral rights, just as all, and only those, who have rights are morally responsible. Moreover, because all persons, and only persons, are morally responsible, Kant believes that all persons, and only persons, have moral rights.

In view of the preceding, it should come as no surprise that Kant denies rights to other-than-human animals. These animals do not have rights because they are not persons. In fact, Kant believes that rational, autonomous beings and animals belong to two distinct, mutually exclusive moral categories; rational, autonomous beings belong to the category *persons*; cows and pigs, coyotes and mink, wrens and eagles belong to a different category, the category (this is Kant's word for it) *things*. When it comes to these animals, therefore, we do nothing wrong when we treat them merely as means. Indeed, for Kant, the reason nonhuman animals exist in the first place is to advance human interests; animals, writes Kant, "are there merely as a means to an end. That end is man." This is why we do nothing wrong to them when we slaughter them for food, trap them for reasons of fashion, or invade their bodies in the name of science. The rights view has very different implications that will be explained in the next chapter.

NONPERSONS AND THE DUTY OF RESPECT

Kant's position, as profound and insightful as I believe it is, and as much as it has influenced my own thinking, is not without its problems, some of them insurmountable, in my judgment. Here I consider only one major difficulty; it concerns which humans count as persons and what follows morally, given Kant's answer.

We begin by noting the obvious: not all that is human is a person, in Kant's sense. A newly fertilized human ovum and a permanently comatose human are human; but neither is what Kant means by person. The same is true of late-term human fetuses, infants, children throughout several years of their lives, and all those human beings, whatever their age, who, for a variety of reasons, lack the intellectual capacities that define Kantian personhood. As such, all these humans lack the morally significant worth possessed by persons. In their case, therefore, no direct duty of respectful treatment is owed and no right to respectful treatment is possessed. Were we to treat these human nonpersons *merely as means*, therefore, Kant would be unable to explain why and how we would be doing anything wrong to them.

I believe that this last proposition expresses a profoundly unacceptable moral position, and I cannot help but believe that people of good will, who are not already committed to some favored ideology, will agree with me. Not for a moment do we believe that it is impossible to do anything wrong to children and the mentally disadvantaged of all ages, for example. Here is another example to consider before rendering judgment, an actual incident involving research using human beings.

The Children of Willowbrook

The Willowbrook State Hospital was a mental hospital (it is now closed) located on Staten Island, New York. For fifteen years, from 1956 to 1971, under the leadership of New York University Professor Saul Krugman, M.D., hospital staff conducted a series of viral hepatitis experiments on thousands of the hospital's severely retarded children, ranging from three to eleven years of age. Among the research questions asked: Could injections of gamma globulin (a complex protein extracted from blood serum) produce long-term immunity to the hepatitis virus?

What better way to find the answer, Dr. Krugman decided, than to separate his subjects into two groups. In one, children were fed the live hepatitis virus and given an injection of gamma globulin; in the other, children were fed the virus but received no injection. In both cases, the virus was obtained from the feces of other Willowbrook children who suffered from the disease.

The results of the experiment were instrumental in leading Dr. Krugman to conclude that hepatitis is not a single disease transmitted by a single virus;

there are, he confirmed, at least two distinct viruses that transmit the infection, what today we know as hepatitis A and hepatitis B, the latter of which is the more severe of the two. Early symptoms include fatigue, loss of appetite, malaise, abdominal pain, vomiting, headache, and intermittent fever; then the patient becomes jaundiced, the urine darkens, the liver swells, and enzymes normally stored in the liver enter the blood. Death results in 1 to 10 percent of cases.

Everyone agrees that many people have benefited from this knowledge and the therapies it made possible. Some historians of biomedical research, it is true, question the necessity of Dr. Krugman's research, citing the comparable findings that Baruch Blumberg made by analyzing blood antigens in his laboratory without subjecting children to the risk of grievous harm. But even if we assume that Dr. Krugman's results could not have been achieved without experimenting on his uncomprehending subjects, the moral case is the same: The purpose of his research was not to benefit each of the children he used, since if injections of gamma globulin did successfully inoculate against hepatitis, as Dr. Krugman suspected, then those children who did not receive injections could not be counted among the possible beneficiaries of his research.

Moreover, it is a perverse moral logic that says, "The children who received the injections of gamma globulin but who did not contract hepatitis—they were the real beneficiaries." Granted, if these children already had the hepatitis virus but failed to develop the disease because of the injections, it would make sense to say that they benefited from Dr. Klugman's experiment. But these children did not already have the virus; they were given the virus by Dr. Klugman and his associates. How can they be described as "beneficiaries"? If I put a bomb in your backpack, armed with an experimental device that I think will defuse the bomb before it is set to go off, and if the device works, I do not think you would shake my hand and thank me because you benefited from my experiment. I think you would (if you could) wring my neck for placing you in grave danger. Would that the children of Willowbrook could have done the same to Dr. Klugman and his associates.

Did Dr. Krugman and his colleagues do anything that showed a lack of respect for these children? One would hope that all humanity with one voice would say yes! Without a doubt he treated these children merely as means in pursuit of knowledge he hoped would benefit others. Given his views, however, Kant cannot make this judgment. Because the duty of respect is owed to persons only, and because these children are not persons, no duty of respect is owed in their case. In fact, in their case, given Kant's theory, *nothing wrong was done to them* when they were treated as they were. The challenge we face is to explain, in a principled, nonarbitrary, nonprejudicial, and rationally defensible way, how the rights view renders a different judgment.

Subjects-of-a-Life

My response to this challenge involves abandoning the Kantian idea that persons are the unique bearers of inherent value and replacing it with an idea for which we have no commonly used word or expression. The absence of such a linguistic marker, referred to by some philosophers as a "lexical gap," is not unique to the present situation. For example, the American philosopher Bill Lawson notes that we do not have a word for the white stringy fiber that clings to bananas. The existence of a lexical gap in this case carries no moral baggage; there is no reason to believe that the absence of a linguistic marker here suggests that moral duties are being shirked, morally important facts ignored. The existence of a lexical gap in other contexts is more problematic. Writing about social policies that affect African Americans, Lawson notes that while some of us "have the concept of the legacy of black subjugation, there is no generally accepted word that denotes this condition." For Lawson, the absence of a commonly used word or expression in this case is symptomatic of a failure to come to terms with a discomforting moral reality. To the extent that what is not named is not worth our serious attention, the absence of a commonly used word or expression with which to talk about "the legacy of black subjugation" suggests that this legacy is unimportant.

I will have more to say about lexical gaps in the next chapter. At this point, I note only that, in the present context, there is something of real moral importance for which we have no commonly used word or expression. *Person* does not fill the gap I have in mind; it covers too few individuals, including too few humans. *Human* does not fill the gap; it covers all humans indiscriminately. Necessity being the mother of invention, I use the words *subject-of-a-life* to fill the gap in question. Let me explain what I mean.

We bring to our lives the mystery of consciousness. Never satisfactorily explained by philosophers or scientists, this fact remains: we are not only in the world, we are aware of it, and aware, too, of what transpires "on the inside," so to speak, in the realm of our feelings, beliefs, and desires. In these respects, we are something more than animate matter, something different from plants; we are the experiencing *subjects-of-a-life*, beings with a biography, not merely a biology. We are *somebodies*, not *somethings*.

These experiential lives we live (and this is also part of the mystery) are unified, not chaotic. In our case, for example, it is not as if the desires we

have belong to someone, the beliefs to someone else, and the feelings to someone totally different; instead, our desires, beliefs, and feelings have a psychological unity; all belong to the distinct individual each of us is; all help define
how the story of our individual lives, our biography, unfolds over time; and
all help illuminate how the story of any one individual's life differs from the
stories of others.

Now, the life of a subject-of-a-life fares experientially better or worse for
the individual whose life it is, logically independently of whether others value
that individual. This does not mean that the quality of our lives is unaffected
by our relationships with others. On the contrary, most of life's most important goods, including love, friendship, the closeness of family, a sense of community, trust, and loyalty depend on the quality of such relationships. The
same is true of most of life's most important evils, including hate, enmity, the
disintegration of family, a sense of alienation, deceit, and betrayal. As a matter
of fact, in short, the quality of our lives waxes and wanes to a considerable
degree depending on whether our relationships with others are amiable and
supportive, the opposite, or somewhere in between. But *that we are individuals who have an experiential welfare*, this is a fact equally true of each of us.
The *kind of being we are—subjects-of-a-life with an experiential welfare*—is
something we all have in common, something we all share equally, something
that makes us all the same, regardless of our gender, intelligence, race, class,
age, religion, birthplace, talent, and social contribution, for example.

This sameness is not morally unimportant. On the contrary, it illuminates
our moral equality. Morally considered, a genius who can play Chopin études
with one hand tied behind her back does not have a "higher" rank than a
seriously mentally impaired child who will never know what a piano is or who
Chopin was. Morally, the rights view does not carve up the world in this way,
placing (after the fashion of Aristotelian moral elitists) the Einsteins in the
"superior" category, above the "inferior" Homer Simpsons of the world. The
less gifted do not exist to serve the interests of the more gifted. The former
are not mere things when compared to the latter, to be used as means to the
latter's ends. From the moral point of view, each of us is equal because each
of us is equally a somebody, not a something, the subject-of-a-life, not a life
without a subject.

Our moral equality clearly does not make us equal in other respects. Homer
Simpson truly is not equally as smart as Albert Einstein, any more than my
poetry is the equal of Galway Kinnell's. Neither is it true that all subjects-of-
a-life have equally rich, equally fulfilling lives. That we are the same in *having
an experiential welfare* does not mean that the *quality of our experiential lives*

is the same. Some are happy; others sad. Some suffer greatly, whether physically or mentally, day in and day out; others hardly know the meaning of the verb *to suffer*. All these differences are real. None is denied by the rights view. The welfare of all those who have an experiential welfare is not the same. What is the same is: we all are somebodies, with an experiential welfare.

In place of Kant's view that *persons* are unique in being inherently valuable, the rights view recognizes the inherent value of all *subjects-of-a-life*. All those who have this status—that is to say, all those who, as subjects-of-a-life, have an experiential welfare—possess inherent value. As such, contrary to Kant, all are owed the direct duty to be treated with respect; and as such, again contrary to Kant, all have an equal right to such treatment. The rights view therefore recognizes moral rights in the case of humans excluded by Kant; the children of Willowbrook, for example. What Dr. Krugman and his colleagues did to those children was wrong for the same reasons that what the researchers did to the men in the Tuskegee syphilis study was wrong. In both cases, the "human guinea pigs" were treated with a lack of respect. In both cases, their right to respectful treatment was violated.

Kant's view excludes more than mentally disadvantaged children. Late-term human fetuses, newborn children, children throughout several years of their lives, and human beings, who, whatever their age and because of various disadvantages, lack the requisite intellectual capacities, are nonpersons. For Kant, therefore, these humans are not owed the duty of respect and lack the right to respectful treatment.

Because the rights view does not limit rights to persons, it recognizes other possibilities. Young children, for example, most certainly are in the world and aware of it; in their case, what happens to them most certainly matters to them, whether anyone else cares about this or not. The same is no less true of older children (recall the teenage rape victim, whose circumstances were described earlier) or adults who make their way through life lacking many of the cognitive capacities we take for granted. Each and all of these humans are subjects-of-a-life; thus do each and all of them share with us the equal right to be treated with respect, according to the rights view.

The situation of newly born and soon to be born humans is more problematic. We are only beginning to understand their psychological complexity; generations of surgeons have operated on them, for example, without using anesthetic, in the belief that *they feel no pain*. A new day is dawning; the more we learn, the more reason we have to attribute feelings, preferences, and desires to prenatal and neonatal humans, capacities that, if present, underpin their independent experiential welfare. Granted, our knowledge here is less secure than in other cases. Granted, perhaps we go too far when we view soon to be born and newly born humans as subjects-of-a-life. Room remains for informed people of good will to disagree. Speaking for myself, because so much is at stake, I would rather err on the side of caution than on the side of excess, meaning: In the absence of compelling evidence to the contrary, I choose to judge and act as if these humans are subjects-of-a-life.

This judgment makes a moral difference. Whereas, given Kant's view, the human nonpersons we have been discussing in principle can be treated as mere means without any wrong being done to them, the rights view reaches the opposite conclusion. To treat any of these humans as if they are of instrumental value only is to do something wrong to them, something that fails to discharge our duty to treat them respectfully, something that violates their right to be treated with respect.

OBJECTIONS TO THE RIGHTS VIEW

Not all is clear sailing for the rights view; like every other moral theory, it faces any number of serious objections that challenge the attribution of rights to humans, independent of any thought about other animals. Four representative objections of this kind will be considered here. (More objections and replies will be found in the works cited in the notes for this section; a variety of objections to the attribution of rights to animals will be considered in chapter 8.)

R. G. Frey makes two important criticisms. First, he criticizes the equality that the rights view attributes to all subjects-of-a-life. He writes:

I do not regard all human life as of equal value. I do not accept that a very severely mentally-enfeebled human or an elderly human fully in the grip of senile dementia or an infant born with only half a brain has a life whose value is equal to that of normal, adult humans. The quality of human life can plummet, to a point where we would not wish *that* life on even our worst enemies; and I see no reason to pretend that a life I would not wish upon even my worst enemies is nevertheless as valuable as the life of any normal, adult human.

It will be noticed that, in the passage just quoted, Frey refers to "the *quality* of human life" and to the fact that "the *quality* of human life" can vary from individual to individual, sometimes "plummet[ing]" to an unquestionably undesirable level. It should be clear, then, that Frey has confused the idea of inherent value with the very different idea of individual welfare. To speak of "quality of life" is to refer to how well an individual's life is faring, while to speak of the "inherent value" of an individual is to refer to the value (the moral status) of the individual whose life it is. Some human subjects-of-a-life are confused, enfeebled, or otherwise disadvantaged. The quality of their lives, let us agree, is less desirable than that of someone who realizes the highest level of human fulfillment. But this does not entail that those with lesser quality of life either have less inherent value or lack inherent value, or that they may, with moral justification, be treated as mere resources by those who have a greater quality of life.

Frey's second criticism also challenges the equality that the rights view attributes to all subjects-of-a-life. "[Not] all human life . . . however deficient, has the same value," he insists. He then goes on to add: "For me, the value of life is a function of its quality, its quality a function of its richness, and its richness a function of its scope or potentiality for enrichment; and the fact is that many humans lead lives of a very much lower quality than ordinary human lives, lives which lack enrichment and where the potentialities for enrichment are severely truncated or absent." Once again, however, Frey's objection is based on misunderstanding. First, the rights view does not state or imply that "all human life . . . has the same value," including the same inherent value (this because not all human beings are subjects-of-a-life); second, while (according to the rights view) all those humans who are subjects-of-a-life have inherent value, and have it equally, it does not follow that the quality of their lives is equal. From the perspective of the rights view, the quality of an individual's life is one thing; the value of the one whose life it is, is another.

A third, distinctively different, objection challenges a form of argument used in the course of making the case for the rights view. The form of argument to which I am referring goes like this:

1. Something is wrong.
2. Such-and-such theory cannot explain why it is wrong.
3. Therefore, the theory is inadequate.

Particular examples of this form of argument include the following:

1. It is wrong to treat some people as slaves.
2. Simple contractarianism is unable to explain why this is wrong.
3. Therefore, simple contractarianism is inadequate.

And, again:

1. It is wrong to murder the innocent in order to benefit others.
2. Utilitarianism is unable to explain why this is wrong.
3. Therefore, utilitarianism is inadequate.

As should be evident, arguments of this type test the adequacy of moral theories by asking how well they conform to our well-considered moral convictions (what philosophers sometimes call "intuitions"). If a theory fails this test, not once but repeatedly, we have reason to believe that we need to look for a better theory

Some philosophers repudiate this form of argument; Singer is among them. He disparages "the in-built conservatism of this approach to ethics, an approach which is liable to make relics of our cultural history as the touch-stones of morality." Why and in what sense does this approach suffer from "in-built conservatism"? Singer reasons as follows:

Our rock bottom moral beliefs are the product of our particular culture's system of values at a given time, together with the influences of our immediate family and social group. These influences, he believes, will tend to be morally conservative because the values imparted will tend to be those that favor the moral status quo. For example, if we had been born into the white propertied class of slave owners in the South prior to the Civil War, the values we would have been taught would have reflected the values of that class and would have been conservative in nature. Instead of being taught values that challenged the moral status quo (for example, that humans are equal regardless of their race) we would have been taught values that fostered it (for example, that blacks are inferior). Once this instruction had taken root, we would have regarded it as "obviously true" that whites are superior to blacks, and this belief would have been incorporated into our body of "moral intuitions."

This argument of Singer's merits two replies. The first is ad hominem. As was remarked in our earlier discussion of his views, the theory he favors (preference utilitarianism) is noteworthy because of *its* in-built conservatism. The American philosopher Dan Brock presses this criticism when he observes:

A person's desires or preferences are the product of biological needs and the socialization process by which she or he is inducted into society, the state, and various social groups. They are importantly determined by and will tend to reinforce the existing social arrangements, power and authority relations, and expectations in one's environment. Consequently, utilitarianism formulated so as to require maximal satisfaction of preferences as they exist, in turn serves to reinforce the existing social structure; it will have a significant conservative bias. For example, a racist, sexist society may foster racist or sexist preferences in its members, and preference utilitarianism seems committed to seeking the satisfaction of these preferences.

Second, and more fundamentally, to test the adequacy of moral theories by asking whether (quoting Singer) "[they] match the data of our settled convictions" need not be conservative in the disparaging sense in which he levels this charge. Beliefs are "conservative" to the extent that they are not subject to alteration. There is, however, no reason to suppose that appeals to our intuitions must be conservative in this sense. Some of our intuitions can be seen to stand in need of revision, once we examine them both in light of new knowledge and in terms of other relevant considerations, including the requirements of elementary justice. For example, many Euro-Americans changed their ideas about how Native Americans should be treated as they came to understand that Native Americans were every bit as human as they were, and people who have a "settled conviction" that discounts the moral status of children can recognize the need to move beyond this conviction once they understand its prejudicial nature. Indeed, as we will see more fully in the next chapter, nothing better demonstrates why using appeals to our intuitions need not foster moral conservatism than the fact that these appeals play an important role in my argument for animal rights. If appeals of this kind were irredeemably conservative, my argument for animal rights could never get beyond endorsing the status quo represented by McDonalds's ubiquitous Golden Arches. (For further discussion of this matter, see the resources cited in the notes accompanying this section.)

A final objection considered here is analogous to the objection I have been pressing against Kant. Given his views, some humans are not persons; given the rights view, some humans (for example, newly fertilized human ova and ancephalic neonates, infants born without a brain or brain activity above the brain stem) are not subjects-of-a-life. Judged on this basis, this objection concludes, they do not have a right to respectful treatment.

Critics might conclude from this that the rights view is unsatisfactory because it denies this right in these cases. Whether this would be a serious defect or not, the rights view does not have this implication. It does not *deny* that these humans lack the right to be treated with respect, or that they lack all other rights. It leaves these questions open. According to the rights view, *all* who are subjects-of-a-life possess inherent value. Whether *only* those who are subjects-of-a-life possess inherent value is a question the rights view does not foreclose. In other words, the rights view allows for the possibility that individuals who are not subjects-of-a-life might nonetheless have a kind of value that is not reducible to instrumental value only. However, the onus of proof will be on those who wish to attribute such value beyond subjects-of-a-life to offer a principled, nonarbitrary, nonprejudicial, and rational defense of doing so, something the rights view itself does not attempt to do.

THE RIGHTS VIEW'S STRENGTHS

It is at this point that the rights view's strengths when compared with Rawlsian contractarianism are most apparent. Rawls's moral outlook has noteworthy virtues. In particular, the prejudicial discrimination against, as well as the permissible exploitation of, those who belong to the "wrong" race, the "wrong" class, or the "wrong" gender, for example, arguably are disallowed by Rawls's veil of ignorance. Given the moral prejudices validated by some of the other views we have considered (simple contractarianism and moral elitism, in particular), Rawls's outlook clearly is superior, and any philosopher working in the areas of moral and political theory owes Rawls an enormous debt of gratitude.

Prejudices linger in the Rawlsian vision nonetheless. Recall that Rawlsian contractors, each of whom must have "a sense of justice," are the only ones to whom direct duties are owed. Because young children and human beings of any age who suffer from quite serious mental disabilities do not satisfy this requirement, no direct duties are owed to them. What duties we have in their case arise because of duties we have to those with a sense of justice.

The rights view preserves the strengths and avoids the weaknesses of Rawlsian contractarianism. It preserves the strengths because it distances itself from prejudicial discrimination against, and the possible exploitation of, members of the extended human family that are based on race, gender, or ethnicity, for example; and it avoids the weaknesses because it denies that one must have a sense of justice in order to be owed direct duties. One has only to ask whether the mentally disadvantaged victim of the gang rape was treated wrongly to realize that Rawls's standard is too high. Without herself having a sense of justice, this unfortunate young girl was treated in ways that give humanity a bad name. Without herself having duties to others, as a subject-of-a-life, *she* was owed the direct duty of respectful treatment; *she* possessed the right to be treated with respect, not some indirect protection grounded in the duties owed to others.

Four final substantive points need to be made before concluding this chapter. First, as was noted in the critical evaluation of utilitarianism, that theory is committed to a procedure that counts all preference satisfactions, no matter from whence they arise. This is why a consistent utilitarianism must count evil preferences, like those of the rapists, as well as those of others who were supportive or complicit, and count their satisfaction as being of equal importance to the comparable preference of their victim. I believe that this procedure is morally obscene; I do not think there is any other word for it. I believe that the preferences of those who violated the young girl, as well as the preferences of those who were supportive or complicit, should play no role whatsoever in the determination of the wrong that was done. The rights view is able to explain why. Evil preferences are those preferences that, when acted upon, either lead agents to violate someone's rights or cause others to approve of, or tolerate, such violations. This is why, according to the rights view, the preferences of the rapists, as well as those who approved of or tolerated what they did, do not count. Not at all.

Second, to act on evil preferences does not mean that those who do so are evil people. People are evil (at least this is the clearest example of what we mean) when, as an expression of their settled personal character, they make a habit of violating others' rights *and* do so cruelly, either by taking pleasure in or by feeling nothing (being indifferent) to the suffering or loss caused by the violation. Contrast this with those who are otherwise decent people but who, in an isolated case, act on preferences that lead them to violate someone's rights, an act that they later regret. This may have been true of some of the teenage rapists. Granted, what they did was horribly wrong; granted, giving in to their evil preferences led them to do it; nevertheless, a single evil act does not a moral monster make. People who do evil (and we all do) often have other redeeming qualities. So even while we are right to judge rights violations to be wrong, we should guard against a rush to judgment concerning the moral character of the violators.

Third, otherwise decent people can be supportive of and complicit in evil as part of their day-to-day lives, not just in isolated incidents. This arguably was true of some white Southerners (and of some white Northerners, too) who benefited from slavery, for example. That great wrongs were done to slaves because their fundamental rights were routinely, often ruthlessly violated is unquestionably true; and that these violations occurred because of the evil preferences of the white majority, that also is unquestionably true. But not all white beneficiaries of slavery were evil people; not all possessed a morally deficient character that led them habitually to enjoy violating others' rights or to regard all violations committed by others with moral indifference. As was observed in the earlier discussion of cruelty-kindness, moral assessments of what people do should be kept distinct from moral assessments of the people who do them. This is a principle that applies in the present case, too. To act on evil preferences, while this is tied to the wrong associated with violating rights, is one thing; to find someone of evil character is another.

Fourth, and finally, the rights view distances itself from those who would encourage or allow nonconsenting sex, including sex with children. The rights view does not say that, when done "in private," there is nothing wrong with "mutually satisfying [sexual] activities" involving adults and children. Rather, we say that there is something wrong in engaging in such activities in the first place. A child cannot give or withhold informed consent. Many cannot even say the words *yes* and *no*. In the nature of the case, engaging in sexual activities with children must be coercive, must display a lack of respect, and thus must be wrong.

In the following chapter I present my argument for animal rights. Before turning to this task, it is worth noting what the rights view offers in the case of human morality. What it offers is a moral theory in which human rights are central; a moral theory that represents the life, the bodily integrity, and the liberty of individuals as being worthy of maximum protection; a moral theory that provides this same protection to all human subjects-of-a-life regardless of their race, gender, class, age, or sophisticated intellectual capabilities, for example; and a moral theory that grounds this equal protection in considerations that are principled, nonarbitrary, nonprejudicial, and rationally defensible.

In chapter 1, I expressed the hope that these pages would demonstrate that my commitment to human rights is, if anything, more central to my thinking than is my commitment to animal rights. I am a human rights advocate (especially for infants, children, and other powerless, vulnerable members of the extended human family) first, an animal rights advocate second. I trust my commitment to human rights has been demonstrated. Even if it should turn out that the conclusions reached in the next chapter are false or foolish, I hope that the conclusions reached in this one, and the arguments used to reach them, because they stand or fall on their own, will be judged accordingly.

7

ANIMAL RIGHTS

We turn now to a consideration of the rights of other-than-human animals. From the outset I have emphasized the cumulative nature of my argument. Whether animals have rights is a topic that cannot profitably be broached before other, more fundamental questions have been answered. These questions include, but are not limited to, questions that critically assess moral theories that deny rights to animals and, as we have seen, sometimes to humans, too. After the weaknesses of these ways of thinking about morality have been reviewed and after it has been explained how the rights view preserves their respective strengths, the reasons for recognizing human rights can be understood; and once these reasons are understood, then—but not before, in my judgment—the reasons why animal rights should be recognized can be understood as well. It has taken this long to arrive at the point where an answer to the question about the rights of animals makes rational sense. Whether the answer I give is or is not correct, the need to approach the issue carefully and fairly, as the previous chapters have attempted to do, demonstrates what was meant when, in chapter 2, I noted that the case for animal rights cannot be given in twenty-five words or less.

Controversial moral issues—and few are more controversial than the one that asks whether animals have rights—characteristically involve four separate but related kinds of questions that help define where and how people can agree or disagree. There are (1) questions of fact; (2) questions of value; (3) questions of logic; and (4) practical questions, those that ask what changes, if any, should be made, given how the other questions have been answered. This chapter explores questions of each kind and explains why the conclusion that other-than-human animals have rights is reached.

QUESTIONS OF FACT

Concerning questions of fact: people of good will who offer opposing answers to controversial moral questions sometimes disagree about what should be done morally because they disagree about what is true factually. For example, some people think it would be morally wrong to legalize active euthanasia, understood as deliberately killing competent, terminally ill patients who suffer greatly and who ask that their lives be ended. Why? One of the reasons given concerns fears about society sliding down a slippery slope. If active euthanasia is legally permitted in a limited number of cases, so this reasoning goes, we will end up legally euthanizing people who are not suffering greatly, who are not terminally ill, and who do not prefer death over remaining alive. To express this concern simply and starkly, these opponents believe that legalizing active euthanasia for some will lead to legalizing murder for others.

But *will* legalizing active euthanasia in some cases lead to murder in others? This is a question of fact, one that illustrates how complicated "mere questions of fact" sometimes can be. With our limited knowledge about the long-term effects of situations, such as the one we find in Holland, where active euthanasia in limited circumstances was legalized in 1973, who is to say with great confidence what the long-term effects of legalization would be?

The central factual questions in the animal rights debate differ in important respects from those that help define the debate over the legalization of active euthanasia. In the latter case, we are being asked to speculate about human behavior in the future; in the former, we are being asked to say what we know about animal psychology here and now. Earlier, in chapter 4, considerations were offered in support of a variety of judgments of fact about animal minds. There it was argued that mammals and birds (at least) have both preference and welfare interests. Despite the Cartesian assertion to the contrary, these animals are our psychological, not merely our biological, kin.

How do we know this? As was noted in that earlier discussion, the grounds for attributing minds to these animals are analogous to those we have for attributing minds to one another. Their behavior resembles our behavior. Their physiology and anatomy resembles ours. And their having a mind, their having a psychology, not only accords with common sense (and with religious teachings without exception), it is supported by our best science. No one of these considerations by itself need be claimed to be proof of animal minds; when taken together, however, they provide compelling grounds for attributing a rich, complex mental life to these other-than-human animals.

QUESTIONS OF VALUE

Questions of value do not concern mere matters of fact, though facts can be highly relevant. This certainly is true in the present case, where one of the central questions of value concerns the moral status of other-than-human animals. Here is what I mean.

The previous chapter included a discussion of subjects-of-a-life. As explained there, subjects-of-a-life not only are in the world, they are aware of it and aware, too, of what transpires "on the inside," in the lives that goes on behind their eyes. As such, subjects-of-a-life are something more than animate matter, something different from plants that live and die; subjects-of-a-life are the experiencing center of *their* lives, individuals who have lives that fare experientially better or worse for themselves, logically independently of whether they are valued by others. At least in the case of mammals and birds, then, the conclusion we reach is simple: as a matter of fact, these animals, as is true in our case, are subjects-of-a-life.

The preceding makes it possible to say something more on the topic of lexical gaps. In general, the traditional vocabulary of moral philosophy has had to make do with three different but related concepts: (1) humans, (2) animals, and (3) persons. No one of the three coincides perfectly with the other two. For example, while it is true that all humans are animals, it is false that all animals are humans; and while it is true that some human beings are persons, in the Kantian sense, no animal beings are. What our language lacks is a commonly used word or expression that applies to the area where humans and animals overlap psychologically. This is the lexical gap "subject-of-a-life" is intended to fill. The introduction of this concept permits us to identify those humans and other animals who share both a family of mental capacities and a common status as beings who have an experiential welfare. The word *human* is inadequate to the task; some subjects-of-a-life are not human. The word *animal* is inadequate to the task; some animals are not subjects-of-a-life. And the word *person* is similarly deficient; some subjects-of-a-life, whether human or not, are not persons. And yet there is no mistaking the reality in question, a reality shared by literally billions of human and animal beings.

If the identity of those who are subjects-of-a-life were morally unimportant, the existence of a lexical gap in the present case would be of no greater moral significance than the existence of a lexical gap in the case of "white stringy fiber that clings to bananas." But the identity of those who are subjects-of-a-life is far from being morally unimportant. On the contrary, for reasons offered in the previous chapter, the idea of being a subject-of-a-life is central to answering the question, "Who is inherently valuable? Who is never to be treated as having instrumental value only?" A more fundamental question of value is difficult to imagine.

As for the suggestion that being a subject-of-a-life illuminates only which *human beings* have inherent value: such a suggestion is symptomatic of the prejudice of speciesism. If what we are being asked to believe is that humans who are subjects-of-a-life are inherently valuable *because they are human beings*, whereas other animals who are subjects-of-a-life lack value of this kind *because they are not human beings*, then what we are being asked to believe, more than suggesting this prejudice, actually embodies it. Just as it is speciesist to count human interests as being morally significant and to deny this same status in the case of the similar interests of nonhumans, because the former are human interests, the latter not, so it is speciesist to affirm inherent value in the case of human subjects-of-a-life and deny this in the case of nonhuman subjects-of-a-life, because the former are humans, the latter not.

What, then, shall we say of the animals who concern us—cows and pigs, coyotes and mink, robins and crows? Are they like us in being subjects-of-a-life? Do they have an experiential welfare that is of importance to them, independently of their possible usefulness to us? Let those with Cartesian inclinations step forward and deny this. The convictions of common sense, in concert with the teachings of the religions of the world and the findings of an informed science, will (as they should) take a contrary view. These animals are our psychological kin. Like us, they bring to their lives the mystery of a unified psychological presence. Like us, they are *somebodies*, not *somethings*. In these fundamental ways, they resemble us, and we, them.

Moreover, and not unimportant, just as the rights view categorically rejects the ranking of human subjects-of-a-life, in terms of those who are "higher" or "superior" compared to those who are "lower" or "inferior," it rejects on grounds of consistency a similar ranking when humans are compared to animals. All human subjects-of-a-life are equal in their morally significant (inherent) value, regardless of how much or little they know, how talented or incompetent they are, how rich or poor they may be, and so on. Only the last vestiges of speciesism could prevent us from reaching the same judgment in the case of animal subjects-of-a-life. *We* are not "higher" or "superior"; *they* are not "lower" or "inferior." In terms of our morally significant, our inherent, value, we are their equals, and they are ours.

QUESTIONS OF LOGIC

Questions of logic ask whether one statement follows from another. There are more or less elaborate methods for determining this; fortunately, their details need not concern us here. Here it is enough to explain how the conclusion that animals have rights follows from a number of other statements for which supporting arguments have been offered in the preceding discussion. By way of summary:

1. Moral theories that deny that we owe direct duties to animals (for example, both simple and Rawls's version of contractarianism) are unsatisfactory. Any plausible moral theory must therefore recognize that animals are owed direct duties. The rights view satisfies this requirement.
2. Moral theories that are speciesist (for example, those that maintain that all, and only, human interests matter morally simply because they are the interests of human beings) are unsatisfactory. Any plausible moral theory must therefore recognize that other-than-human interests matter morally. The rights view satisfies this requirement.
3. Moral theories that attempt to explicate the direct duties we owe to animals by reference to human character traits (for example, the cruelty-kindness view) are unsatisfactory. Any plausible moral theory must therefore be able to distinguish between moral assessments of what people do and the moral character they display in doing it. The rights view satisfies this requirement.
4. Moral theories that attempt to explicate human morality while dispensing with the idea of moral rights (for example, preference utilitarianism) are unsatisfactory. Any plausible moral theory must therefore recognize the rights of humans, including the right to respectful treatment in particular. The rights view satisfies this requirement.
5. Moral theories that attempt to explicate human morality by attributing inherent value to all and only those humans who are persons (for example, Kant's position) are unsatisfactory. Any plausible moral theory must therefore recognize the inherent value of humans who are not persons. The rights view satisfies this requirement.
6. Moral theories that deny that no other-than-human animals have an experiential welfare (for example, Carruthers's position) are unsatisfactory. Any plausible moral theory must therefore recognize that there are other-than-human animals who have an experiential welfare. The rights view satisfies this requirement.
7. Moral theories that attempt to limit inherent value to all, and only, humans who are subjects-of-a-life, thereby denying this same value to other animals who are subjects-of-a-life, are speciesist and unsatisfac-

tory. Any plausible moral theory must therefore recognize that anyone with an experiential welfare matters morally, whatever their species. The rights view satisfies this requirement.

8. Moral theories that affirm inherent value and rights in the case of humans who are subjects-of-a-life are preferable to positions that deny this. The rights view satisfies this requirement.

With statements 1 through 8 serving as the argument's foundation, the rights view's case for animal rights concludes as follows:

9. Because the relevant similarity shared by humans who have inherent value is that we are subjects-of-a-life, in the sense explained; because the nonhuman animals who concern us are like us in that they, too, are subjects-of-a-life; and because relevantly similar cases should be judged similarly; it follows that these nonhuman animals also possess inherent value.

10. Because all those who possess inherent value possess the equal right to be treated with respect, it follows that all those human beings *and* all those animal beings who possess inherent value share the equal right to respectful treatment.

Does this constitute a "strict proof" of animal rights? My answer here echoes my answer to the earlier question about arguments for human rights. Strict proofs are not possible in these quarters. What can be done, and what I have attempted to do, is to explain how the ascription of rights to animals is supported by a way of thinking about morality that is principled, nonarbitrary, nonprejudicial, and rationally defensible—one that both preserves the strengths and avoids the weaknesses of the influential moral theories examined along the way. Short of constructing a strict proof, my argument here again functions to shift the burden of appropriate proof to those who favor some other view, meaning: it will be the burden of others, who disagree with the conclusions I reach, to explain where and why my argument goes wrong, or how some other moral theory has better reasons, stronger arguments on its side.

PRACTICAL QUESTIONS

From the outset I have noted the abolitionist character of my views, both in the case of animal rights and regarding the animal rights movement. "This movement," I noted, "seeks not to reform how animals are exploited, making what we do to them more humane, but to abolish their exploitation—to end it, completely." Why humane reforms are not enough should be clear. In the case of the use of animals in science, for example, the rights view is categorically abolitionist. Animals are not our tasters. We are not their kings. Because animals used in research are routinely, systematically treated as if their value is reducible to their usefulness to others, they are routinely, systematically treated with a lack of respect; thus are their rights routinely, systematically violated. This is just as true when they are used in studies touted as holding real promise of human benefits as it is when they are used in trivial, duplicative, unnecessary, or unwise research. We cannot justify routinely harming or killing human beings for these sorts of reasons. Neither can we do so in the case of nonhuman animals in a laboratory. It is not refinement in research protocols that is called for; not mere reduction in the number of animals used; not more generous use of anesthetic or the elimination of multiple surgery; not reforms in an institution that is possible only at the price of systematic violations of animal rights. Not larger cages, empty cages. Total abolition. The best we can do when it comes to using animals in science is not to use them. This is where our duty lies, according to the rights view.

As for commercial animal agriculture, the rights view takes a similar abolitionist position. The fundamental moral wrong here is not that animals are kept in stressful close confinement or in isolation, or that their pain and suffering, their needs and preferences are ignored or discounted. All these are wrong, of course, but they are not the fundamental wrong. They are symptoms and effects of the deeper, systematic wrong that allows these animals to be viewed and treated merely as means to human ends, as resources for us—indeed, as renewable resources. Giving animals on farms more space, more natural environments, more companions does not right the fundamental wrong, any more than giving animals in laboratories more anesthesia or bigger, cleaner cages would right the fundamental wrong in their case. Nothing less than the total dissolution of commercial animal agriculture will do this, just as, for similar reasons, the rights view requires nothing less than the total eradication of the fur industry. The rights view's abolitionist implications, as I have said, are both clear and uncompromising.

That beliefs such as these will be seen by many people as radical and extreme is not a judgment I have sought to avoid; given the dominant customs of the culture in which we live, these beliefs cannot be perceived in any other way. To say that animals have rights means something more than that we should be nice to them. Given that they, like us, are protected by invisible No

Trespassing signs; and given that respect for their rights, as is true in our case, trumps any private or public interest we might have, however important that interest might be, the "radical," "extreme" abolitionist implications of the rights view are unavoidable. Morally, we are never to take the life, invade or injure the body, or limit the freedom of any animal who is a subject-of-a-life, just because we personally or society in general will benefit. If we mean anything by the ascription of rights to animals, we mean this.

One final point. Contrary to the implications of utilitarianism, bestiality finds no justification within the rights view. The rights view does not say that, when done "in private," there is nothing wrong with "mutually satisfying [sexual] activities" involving humans and animals. Rather, it says that there is something wrong in engaging in such activities in the first place. An animal cannot give or withhold informed consent. An animal cannot say yes. Or "no." In the nature of the case, for humans to engage in sexual activities with animals must be coercive, must display a lack of respect, thus must be wrong.

In reaching this judgment, the rights view is not paying irrational homage to outdated sexual taboos or endorsing sexual prudishness. Engaging in "mutually satisfying [sexual] activities" is one of life's finest pleasures. By all means, then, the more such activities, the better . . . *provided* that those who participate are able to give or withhold their informed consent. The end of sexual satisfaction never justifies the means of sexual coercion.

8

OBJECTIONS AND REPLIES

Many people resist the idea of animal rights. General objections, as I call them, are the stuff of everyday incredulity; for a variety of reasons, some people find it hard to believe that animals have rights. Other people dismiss animal rights for religious reasons, and not a few philosophers reject animal rights on philosophical grounds. Representative objections of each kind are considered in this chapter.

GENERAL OBJECTIONS

"Animals Are Not Human."

People who reject animal rights sometimes do so by stating the obvious: other-than-human animals are not human. From this they infer that animals do not have rights. Part of what this objection alleges certainly is true. Dogs and dolphins, rhinoceroses and roosters are not human beings. While true, this fact provides no reason for thinking that animals do not have rights.

The most reasonable interpretation of the "Animals are not human" objection is that animals do not have rights because animals are not members of our species—the human species, the species *Homo sapiens*. However, truths like this one (biological truths) have no moral import. All they tell us is that some beings (human beings) belong to one biological species, while other beings (wolf beings, for example) belong to another biological species. But who belongs to what species is not relevant to thinking about morality. If we think humans have rights but wolves lack them, this is not just because we belong to different species.

A second reply notes that moral rights can never justifiably be denied for prejudicial reasons. Race is such a reason. Gender is such a reason. The same is true of species membership. To suppose that what species one belongs to determines whether one has rights bespeaks a prejudice of the same kind as racism and sexism; it bespeaks speciesism.

"Belief in Animal Rights Is Absurd."

Some critics challenge the idea of animal rights head-on. The idea is absurd, they say, because it is foolish to believe that animals have a right to vote, to marry, and to change their citizenship. Thus, animals have no rights.

Part of what is said here is true: any view that entails that animals have the right to vote, to marry, and to change their citizenship is absurd. The rights view helps us understand why belief in animal rights does not have these absurd implications. Different individuals do not have to have *all* of the same rights in order to have *some* of the same rights. An eight-month-old child, for example, does not have the right to vote. But this does not mean that the child lacks the right to be treated with respect. On the contrary, young children possess this right, at least according to the rights view. And since these children possess this right, without having all rights, there is no reason to judge the status of animals differently. Cows and crows do not need to have the right to vote in order to have the right to be treated with respect.

"Amoeba Rights!"

A common criticism of animal rights attempts to reduce the idea to absurdity in another way. The criticism alleges that if *any* nonhuman animal has rights, then *every* nonhuman animal has rights. Thus, since it is absurd to believe that amoebas have rights, it must be no less absurd to believe that ducks and dolphins have rights.

Is it absurd to believe in amoeba rights? "Absurd" might be too harsh a word. "False" is more temperate and expresses my thinking. Why? Because I have no good reason to believe that such simple forms of animate life are subjects-of-a-life and very good reasons (for example, reasons based on comparative anatomy and physiology) for believing that they are not. Thus, the rights view offers principled grounds for believing in the rights of some nonhuman animals without our having to believe in the rights of all nonhuman animals, amoebas included.

Note, as well, how this objection invites the following parallel argument:

If any animal has rights, then all animals (including amoebas) have rights.
Human animals have rights.
Therefore, all animals (including amoebas) have rights.

Without a doubt, people who press the "amoeba objection" to animal
rights would distance themselves from this parallel argument. No less certainly, they will have a difficult time justifying why they do so without falling
back on one or another objection (for example, "Animals are not humans")
that fail for independent reasons.

"What about Plants?"

If my experience is any guide, this is the most common objection to animal
rights. The logic that drives the question is simple. If animals have rights,
then so do plants. And if plants have rights, then it must be just as wrong to
eat a spinach salad as it is to eat a sirloin steak—a relief to the troubled meat
eater, a terrible cross to bear for the conscientious vegetarian.

As is true of the "Amoeba rights!" objection, the rights view has a principled response. Inherent value belongs equally to all who are subjects-of-a-life,
individuals who (as I have explained) are in the world and aware of the world.
Moreover, what happens to them matters to them because it makes a difference to their experiential welfare. You and I are subjects-of-a-life. So are cows
and pigs. In the case of plants, however, we have no good reason to affirm,
and abundantly good reason to deny, that they are "somebodies." Are they
alive? Yes. Are they the subjects-of-a-life? No.

"But isn't it possible that all living beings have equal inherent value?" The
rights view concedes this possibility; it does not silence those philosophers
(Paul Taylor, for example) who argue for a more radical egalitarianism. I note
only that a principled, nonarbitrary, nonprejudicial, rational defense must be
offered by any philosopher who embraces such a view, something that, in my
judgment, has not been done to date.

Note as well why "plant rights" would not remove the obligation to abstain
on principle from eating the flesh of animals. Cows who are turned into ham-
burgers and pigs who are served as ribs have to eat an awful lot of grain and
other plants before they go to slaughter. Paradoxically, the best way to minimize our destruction of plant life (assuming we continue to eat at all) is to eat
as low on the food chain as possible, something we fail to do if we eat meat.

Whatever may be true of plants, this we know: the billions of animals who,
in our culture, are routinely eaten, trapped, and used in laboratories are like

us in being subjects-of-a-life. Thus, since we must recognize *our* equal inherent value and *our* equal right to be treated with respect, reason compels us to recognize *their* equal inherent value and *their* equal right to be treated with respect. A prudent morality enjoins us to act on what is true, not on what might be.

"Animals Do Not Understand Rights."

Sometimes critics point out that animals do not understand what rights are, from which they conclude that animals do not have any. This argument leaves a good deal to be desired. In my own case, for example, after having thought about rights for more than thirty years, I am certain that I still do not fully understand them. Moreover, I am quite certain that the children of Willowbrook, as well as all children throughout many years of their lives, do not understand rights at all. Yet we do not say (and we should not say) that they have no rights, whether rights to bodily integrity and to life, in particular, or the right to be treated with respect, in general. Neither can we consistently argue, therefore, that animals lack these rights because they do not understand what rights are.

"Animals Do Not Respect Our Rights."

Critics of animal rights sometimes maintain that animals cannot have rights because animals do not respect our rights. Again, part of this objection is correct: animals do not respect our rights. Animals (we have every good reason to believe) have no idea of what it means to respect someone's rights. Once again, however, the moral status of young children should serve to remind us of how unfounded the requirement of reciprocity is. We do not suppose that young children must first respect our rights before we are duty bound to respect theirs. Reciprocity is not required in their case. There is no nonarbitrary, nonprejudicial reason to demand that animals must conform to a different standard.

"Animals Eat Other Animals."

Sometimes an objection to animal rights addresses a particular practice, such as meat eating. Critics point out that lions eat gazelles, then ask how it can be wrong if we eat chickens. The most obvious difference in the two cases is that lions *have* to eat other animals in order to survive. We do not. So what a lion *must* do does not logically translate into what we *may* do. Besides, it is worth noting how much this objection diverges from our normal practice. Most Americans live in houses that have central heating and indoor plumbing, ride in cars and wear clothes. Other animals do not do any of these things. Should we therefore stop living as we live and start imitating them? Should we go feral, leaving our home and our clothes behind? I know of no critic of animal rights who advocates anything remotely like this. Why, then, place what carnivorous animals eat in a unique category as being the one thing animals do that we should imitate?

"Where Do You Draw the Line?"

Critics sometimes challenge animal rights by asking, "Where do you draw the line? How do you know *exactly* which animals are subjects-of-a-life and which animals are not?" There is an honest answer to these vexing questions: We do not know *exactly* where to draw the line. Consciousness, which is common to all those who are subject-of-a-life, is one of life's great mysteries. Whether or not mental states are identical with brain states, we have massive evidence that having any mental states at all presupposes having an intact, functioning central nervous system and brain activity above the brain stem. Where exactly this physiological basis for consciousness emerges on the phylogenic scale, where exactly it disappears, no one can really know with certainty.

But neither do we need to know this. We do need to know exactly how tall a person must be to be tall, before we can know that Shaq O'Neal is tall. We do not need to know exactly how old a person must be to be old, before we can know that Grandma Moses was old. Similarly, we do not need to know exactly where an animal must be located on the phylogenic scale to be a subject-of-a-life, before we can know that the animals who concern us—the mammals and birds who are raised to be eaten, those who are ranched or trapped for their fur, or those who are used as models of human disease, for example—are subjects-of-a-life. We do not need to know everything before we can know something. Our ignorance about how far down the phylogenic scale we should go before we say that consciousness vanishes should not prevent us from saying where it is obviously present.

RELIGIOUS OBJECTIONS

As was noted at the beginning of this chapter, sometimes some people object to animal rights for religious reasons. Without making any claim to completeness, the main religious objections to animal rights include the following:

"Animals Do Not Have Souls."

This common objection ties possession of rights to future prospects of life after death. If animals lack souls, there is no life beyond the grave for them. When their bodies die, the somebody who they were is totally annihilated. It is worth noting that not all religions agree on this point. Hinduism and many Native American traditions are obvious counterexamples; even mainstream Christian theologians (John Wesley provides one example) find Biblically based arguments in favor of the souls of animals.

But let us assume, for the sake of argument, that animals do not have immortal souls. Two points need to be made, the first logical, the second theological. Concerning the logical: Who does or does not have an immortal soul has no logical bearing on who does or does not have rights. Who does or does not have a soul is relevant to answering the question, "What happens to X after X dies?" Questions that ask who has rights, by contrast, have nothing to do with what happens after someone dies; these questions concern the moral status individuals have while they are alive. Asking who has an immortal soul is as logically irrelevant to asking who has rights as asking who has blond hair or missing teeth.

Theologically, it would be perverse to teach that, because animals do not have lives after they die, we are free to make sure they are miserable while they are alive. If anything, a credible theology would teach *exactly the opposite*. Because animals do not have a life after they die, we should do everything in our power to ensure that this, their only life, is as long and good as possible. Since this is an important idea, let me explain it more fully.

Terrible things sometimes happen to good people. Job, for example. His crops fail. His family dies. His reputation is destroyed. Even so, if Job has an immortal soul, a day may come when all his earthly travails are more than compensated for by the bliss that awaits him in heaven. This can never happen to animals, if they lack immortal souls. For them, there is no heavenly bliss, no future compensation. For them, there is only this life and nothing more. Do we therefore say, "We are free to do just about anything we want to do to them while they are alive?" Or do we say, as those who believe in animal rights would say, "We should do everything in our power to ensure that this, their only life, is as long and good as possible?" If the object of one's belief is a loving God, not a sadistic one, the questions answer themselves.

"God Gave Rights Only to Human Beings."

This is the most common religious basis of human rights. The idea seems simple enough. Limited in power as we are, we cannot create moral rights.

Unlimited in power as God is, God can. Indeed, not only can God do this, God actually saw fit to do so, which is why we have the rights we do.

This way of thinking will not find favor among agnostics and atheists. If our rights can only be understood as a gift from God, people who do not believe in God (atheists), as well as those who do not know what to believe (agnostics), could not consistently believe in human rights. Yet many of these people do believe in them, some, most fervently. Are we to say that they must be mistaken, that it is impossible for humans to have rights without God having given them to us? This is not something atheists and agnostics are likely to take lying down.

Dissatisfaction with this way of thinking is not limited to nonbelievers by any means. Even the most devout amongst us will have well-considered reasons for being critical. This can be explained by using Christianity as our working example.

Some Christians no doubt believe that God is the source of our rights. After all, didn't America's founding fathers (some of whom were not Christians, by the way) say that we were "endowed by our Creator with certain unalienable rights"? If we cannot trust the founding fathers, whom can we trust?

Whatever might be true in other regards, the founding fathers are not reliable guides in this one. We do well to remember that these are the same people whose God distributed rights with startling prejudice. Their God did not give rights to women, or to slaves, or to Native Americans, or to children, or to the mentally disadvantaged, or to white men lacking property. Their God saw fit to distribute rights in ways that advantaged white men of property and disadvantaged everyone else. How convenient for the founding fathers to have God on their side! If asked to illustrate how prejudice operates, it would be difficult to find a better and, at the same time, a worse example. Great people are not above making great mistakes.

Simple prudence counsels that we look for wise guidance elsewhere. What better place to look (in the present context) than the Bible? When we do, here is what we find—or, rather, here is what we do not find. We do not find anyplace in the Bible where God gives rights to humans. In no chapter, in no verse, do we read that God says (for example): "I hereby give rights to humans even as I withhold them from animals!" The truth of the matter is, we simply do not find anything remotely like this in the Bible.

What we do find is something semantically and morally different. The Biblical ethic, especially the one we find in the New Testament, is an ethic of love (*agapē*), not an ethic of rights. Our existence is a gift of God's abundant love, and the love we are commanded to have for our neighbors is something

CHAPTER 8

we freely give, after the model of God's love for us, not something our neighbor is entitled to demand from us, as a matter of justice. Our obligation to love our neighbor is not based on our neighbor's right to be loved. Within the Biblical framework, my saying "I have a right to your *agapē*!" reflects as much confusion as my saying to Bill Gates, "I have a right to your money!" People who credit the God of the Bible with being the source of our rights are guilty of reading into the Bible what they want to be there rather than accepting what actually is said.

"Well, at Least God Gave Us Dominion."

People of a religious bent, especially Christians who take the Bible seriously, often agree that rights are not the moral currency of their faith-based ethic. You just don't find them in the Bible. What you do find, very unambiguously, is that God gives us dominion over the animals, pronounced most famously in these words:

> And God said, "Let us make man in our image, after our likeness: and let them have dominion over the fish of the sea, and over the fowl of the air, and over the cattle, and over all the earth, and over every creeping thing that creepeth upon the earth." So God created man in his own image, in the image of God created he him; male and female created he them. And God blessed them, and God said unto them, "Be fruitful, and multiply, and replenish the earth, and subdue it: and have dominion over the fish of the sea, and over the fowl of the air, and over every living thing that moveth upon the earth" (Genesis 1:26–27, King James Version).

What could be clearer than that other animals were created for our use? What could be clearer than that we therefore do nothing wrong when we limit their freedom, injure their bodies, or take their lives to satisfy our needs and desires?

This is not how I read the Bible. To be given dominion by God is not to be given a blank check made out to satisfying our needs and desires. On the contrary, it is to be charged with the awesome responsibility of being the creator's agent within creation; in other words, we are called upon by God to be as loving and caring for what God has created as God was loving and caring in creating it. Indeed, as I understand the idea, this is what it means to be "created in God's image."

Myself, I do not know how anyone can read the opening account of creation in Genesis (one can take this seriously without taking it literally) and come away with a different understanding of God's plans for and hopes in creation. God, you may recall, creates the other animals on the same day (the sixth) as Adam and Eve. I read in this representation of the order of creation a prescient recognition of the vital kinship humans share with other animals. More than this, I find in this opening saga an even deeper, more profound message. God *did not* create animals for our use—not for our entertainment, not for our scientific curiosity, not for our sport, not even for our food. On the contrary, the nonhuman animals currently exploited in these ways were created to be just what they are: *independently good* expressions of the divine love that, in ways that are likely to remain forever mysterious to us, was expressed in God's creative activity. To the extent that we strive to act to honor, protect, and love God's good creations, we will act in ways that are indistinguishable from those who strive to respect the rights of animals. Thus, though we do not find the notion of moral rights in the Bible, there is a way to read its pages that yields the same "radical" and "extreme" views associated with the philosophy of animal rights.

"Not even for our food?" I can hear the skeptic mutter. "Is that a misprint?" To which my answer is, "No, it is not a misprint. It's what the Bible teaches." The "meat" we are given by God for our food is not the flesh of animals; here is what it is: "And God said, 'Behold, I have given you every herb bearing seed, which is upon the earth, and every tree, in which is the fruit of a tree yielding seed; to you it shall be meat'" (Genesis 1:29). The message could not be any clearer. In the most perfect state of creation, in the Garden of Eden, humans are vegans. So if we ask what God hoped for "in the beginning," when it comes to our food the answer is not open to dispute. It was not a diet of Big Macs and cheese omelets.

For Christians, then, the question asked each day is a simple one. "Do I try to turn my life around and begin my journey back to Eden—back to a more loving relationship with this gift of creation? Or do I continue to live in ways that increase my distance from what God hoped for?" This is a question that is answered in many different ways, not one only. There is no argument there. But neither should we argue over whether one way Christians answer this question is with the choices they make about the food on their plate.

PHILOSOPHICAL OBJECTIONS

Carl Cohen, whose ideas have been mentioned along the way and whose defense of speciesism was examined in chapter 3, is the most vocal and famous philosophical critic of animal rights. It will be appropriate, therefore, if his critical arguments are treated as representative of philosophical objections to animal rights.

Before beginning, I note that Cohen and I are of one mind on a number of important matters. Not only do we agree that rights are valid claims, we also agree that rights are trump. "Rights always trump interests," he writes at one point. What this means is not obscure. If I have a right to life, then you are not morally entitled to kill me because you stand to benefit. My right trumps your interests. The same is true of society at large: my life is not to be taken in pursuit of improvements in the general welfare. In Cohen's view, as in mine, the rights of the individual trump the otherwise noble goal of advancing the good of society.

But do all humans have rights? And do all animal lack them? Cohen answers yes to the first question, yes to the second. I restrict my comments here to the arguments he offers in support of his answer to the second question. A fuller body of criticism will be found in the works cited in the notes for this section.

Cohen's First Objection

Cohen's first objection rests on the amorality of animals, an idea he introduces after asking us to imagine a lioness who kills a baby zebra. He writes:

> Do you believe the baby zebra has the *right* not to be slaughtered? Or that the lioness has the *right* to kill that baby zebra to feed her cubs? Perhaps you are inclined to say, when confronted by such natural rapacity (duplicated in various forms millions of times each day on planet earth), that *neither* is right or wrong, that neither the zebra nor the lioness has a right against the other. Then I am on your side. Rights are pivotal in the moral realm and must be taken seriously, yes; but zebras and lions and rats do not live in a moral realm; their lives are totally amoral. There *is* no morality for them; animals do no moral wrong, ever. In their world there are no wrongs and there are no rights.

The essential points being argued here, insofar as they concern animal rights, may be summarized as follows:

The Amorality-Rights Argument

1. Animals live in an amoral world (a world where nothing is right or wrong).

2. Those who live in an amoral world cannot have rights against one another.
3. Therefore, animals cannot have rights against one another.

Some philosophers (Steve Saponsitz, for example) challenge the assumption that animals are incapable of moral agency. I side with Cohen on this matter. In particular, we both deny that the baby zebra has a right not to be killed by the lioness and that the lioness has a right to kill the baby zebra. This much granted, what may we logically conclude? It is in our respective answer to this question that Cohen and I part company.

What follows, Cohen believes, is that animals cannot have rights against us. In other words, because animals, living as they do in an amoral world, cannot have rights against one another, we must conclude, he thinks, that animals "[have] no rights that [we] can possibly infringe." Thus we have:

4. If animals cannot have rights against one another, they cannot have rights against us.
5. Therefore, animals cannot have rights against us.

Something has gone wrong here. To understand why, consider an argument having the same logical structure as the Amorality-Rights Argument, only this one dealing with duties.

The Amorality-Duties Argument

1. Animals live in an amoral world (a world where nothing is right or wrong).
2. Those who live in an amoral world cannot have duties to one another.
3. Therefore, animals cannot have duties to one another.
4. If animals cannot have duties to one another, we cannot have duties to them.
5. Therefore, we cannot have duties to animals.

Because of the conclusions reached in the critical examination of indirect duty views in chapter 4, we know that statement 5 is false. As a matter of logic, therefore, we know that not all the other statements in this argument can be true. The culprit obviously is statement 4. Just because animals cannot have duties to one another, it does not follow that we cannot have duties to them.

Logically, the possibility of nonhuman animals having rights is no different. From the fact that animals cannot have rights against one another, it does not follow that they cannot have rights against us. I think they can and do. Cohen thinks they cannot and do not. Who is correct is open to debate. What is not open to debate is whether the issue can be resolved by establishing that animals cannot have rights against one another.

Cohen's Second Objection

Cohen's second objection denies rights to animals because they are not the right kind of being. By contrast, humans (all of us) are. Writes Cohen: "[H]umans are of a kind that rights pertain to them as humans." If we can decipher what this means, we might better understand what drives the argument. One thing it cannot mean is that all humans are the same biologically— that, for example, all humans, and only humans, belong to the same species. As was explained above, from "All, and only, humans are *Homo sapiens*," nothing follows concerning our moral status, least of all that "humans are of a kind that rights pertain to them because they are human."

But if it is not some universal, unique biological fact, what is there about being human that might ground our universally shared, our unique, moral status? Cohen's answer will be found in his assertion that "humans live lives that will be, have been, or remain *essentially* moral" (emphasis in original). To say that the lives humans live are *essentially* moral means that we could not live human lives if we did not live our lives as moral beings. In other words, being in the world as a moral being, unlike being in the world as a male or female, a student or teacher, a plumber or philosopher is so central to living a human life that, absent the capacities required for living a moral life, a person cannot live a human life.

This view is not without its attractions. To exercise our moral capacities—to involve ourselves in moral deliberation and to take responsibility for our actions, for example—arguably is necessary if we are to live human lives. Certainly this is true of those who read these words, utilizing, as we do, our moral capacities everyday of our lives. Moreover, in the case of infants who have the potential to exercise these capacities, it is undeniably true that, barring incapacitating injury or premature death, they will use these capacities in the future. And as for those who, though presently senile or comatose, once lived their lives as we live ours: they most certainly used these same capacities in the past. Thus would it seem that Cohen thinks truly when he writes that "human beings live lives that will be, or have been, or remain *essentially* moral."

I believe this is a fair interpretation of Cohen's argument, an interpretation that is supported by what he writes and the spirit in which he writes it, and one that may be summarized as follows:

The Right-Kind Argument

1. Individuals have rights if, and only if, they are a kind of being whose lives will be, have been, or remain essentially moral.
2. All, and only, humans (at least among terrestrial beings) are this kind of being.
3. Therefore, all, and only, humans (at least among terrestrial beings) have rights.
4. Other animals are not human.
5. Therefore, other animals do not have rights.

Once we understand the content and structure of the argument, we can begin to recognize where and why it goes wrong. An obvious place to begin is with the argument's first premise: "Individuals have rights if, and only if, they are a kind of being whose lives will be, have been, or remain essentially moral." Even if we grant that all humans have rights because they are the "right kind" of being, it does not follow that *only* humans have them. The central question in dispute asks, "Do *animals* have rights?" That morality is essential to human life *leaves every question open* regarding the moral status of animals. That humans will be, have been, or are morally responsible for their actions *leaves every question open* regarding the identity of those to whom we are responsible. In short, even if morality is essential to human but not to animal life, and even if all humans have rights because of this essential aspect of our being, it does not follow that only humans have rights.

Cohen's Third Objection

Cohen has another argument against animal rights. Unlike the Amorality-Rights Argument, which rests on the amoral condition of nonhuman animals, and unlike the Right-Kind Argument, which rests on essential features of being human, this argument is grounded in how and where rights arise. "[R]ights," Cohen declares, "are *universally* human, arise in the human realm, apply to humans generally" (emphasis in original). Other animals, alas, are not "members of [this] community," except in some extended or meta-phorical sense, which is why they lack rights. Bring forth whatever impressive list of capacities and achievements one might wish (communicative skills among nonhuman primates, the cleverness of cats, the sagacity of scrub jays); compare these animals with a human bereft of all cognitive and volitional abilities; it matters not. The human has rights, the other animals do not. "It is beside the point to insist that animals have remarkable capacities," Cohen observes, in one of his essays,

> that they really have a consciousness of self, or of the future, or make plans, and so on. And the tired response that because infants plainly cannot make moral claims they must have no rights at all, or that rats must have them too, we ought forever put aside. Responses like these arise out of a misconception of right itself. They mistakenly suppose that rights are tied to some identifiable individual capacities, or sensibilities, and they fail to see that rights arise only in a community of moral beings, and that therefore there are spheres in which rights do apply and spheres in which they do not.

Despite a certain lack of clarity, I take it that the decisive criterion that Cohen is proposing for possessing rights is not whether one understands what rights are, not whether one can claim them, and so on; it is whether one is a member of the community in which rights arise. Since the only community in which they arise, at least in the terrestrial sphere, is the community comprised of human beings, being human is both a necessary and sufficient condition of possessing rights. Thus we have:

The Community Argument

1. All, and only, those individuals have rights who are members of communities in which the idea of rights arises.
2. Within the terrestrial sphere, the idea of rights arises only in the human community.
3. Therefore, within that sphere, all, and only, humans have rights.
4. Animals are not members of the human community.
5. If animals are not members of the human community, they have no rights.
6. Therefore, animals have no rights.

This argument will not withstand a moment's critical scrutiny. Conceptually, there is a distinction between (1) the origin of an idea and (2) the scope of an idea. The former concerns how (to use Cohen's word) the idea *arises*; the latter concerns the range of objects or individuals to which or to whom the idea may be intelligibly applied. The central point to recognize is that these two matters are logically distinct: The scope of an idea is something that must be determined independently of considerations about the origin of an idea.

By way of example: As far as we know, ideas like "central nervous system" and "genes" arise only among humans because only humans have the requisite cognitive capacities to form them. But the range of entities to which these ideas apply is not necessarily limited to all and only members of the community in which they originate. Indeed, not only is the scope of these ideas not necessarily limited to all and only humans, there are literally billions of non-human animals to whom the ideas actually apply—who have, that is, both genes and a central nervous system.

Considered conceptually, discussions regarding rights are no different. We grant that, as far as we know, the idea of rights arises only among humans because only humans live in the requisite kind of community and have the requisite cognitive capacities. But the range of entities to which this idea applies is not necessarily limited to members of the community in which the idea originates. Logically, one might as well infer that wolves cannot have genes or that dogs lack a central nervous system because these animals do not belong to a community in which these ideas arise. The Community Argument therefore fails to prove that no animal has rights.

All things fairly considered, then, Cohen's objections are deficient. Despite the subtlety and influence of his ideas, his arguments fail to offer a serious challenge to belief in animal rights.

CONCLUSION

Many are the objections to animal rights—too many for any one person to consider at any one time. Those that have been considered in this chapter are not the weakest or least influential by any means. On the contrary, they are representative of the best thinking one finds among the large body of general, religious, and philosophical objections. None succeeds, I believe, for the reasons given. To the extent that our confidence in a moral theory's adequacy increases, the more the theory's central tenets withstand fair criticism, then the more the defense offered in this chapter should serve to increase our confidence in the rights view.

9

MORAL PHILOSOPHY AND CHANGE

Whether the ways animals are treated by humans adds to the evil of the world depends not only on how they are treated but also on what their moral status is. Not surprisingly, the rights view represents the world as containing far more evil than it is customary to acknowledge. First, and most obviously, there is the evil associated with the ordinary, day-to-day treatment to which literally billions of animals are subjected. Representative examples from the food industry, the fashion industry, and the research industry were summarized in chapter 2; as has been mentioned before, additional documentation of their systematic abuse will be found in the resources mentioned at the end of the preface. If it is true, as has been argued, that these animals have a right to be treated with respect, then the massive day-to-day invasion of their bodies, denial of their basic liberties, and destruction of their very lives suggests a magnitude of evil so vast that, like light years in astronomy, it is all but incomprehensible.

But this is not the end of the matter. The magnitude of evil is much greater than the sum of the violations of animal rights, the morally wrong assaults on their independent value these violations represent, and the incalculable pain and deprivation animals are made to endure. Recall that one of the weaknesses of preference utilitarianism is that it must count evil preferences in the process of reaching a fully informed judgment of moral right and wrong. This is a weakness that any plausible moral outlook must avoid, and the rights view has a way of doing so. As was noted near the end of chapter 6, according to the rights view, evil preferences are those preferences that, when acted upon, either lead agents to violate someone's rights or cause others to approve of, or tolerate, such violations.

From the perspective of the rights view, therefore, the magnitude of the evil in the world is not represented only by the evil done to animals when their rights are violated; it includes as well the innumerable human preferences that are satisfied by doing so. That the majority of people who act on such preferences (for example, people who earn a living in the fur industry or those who frequent Colonel Sanders) do not recognize the preferences that motivate them as evil—indeed, that some will adamantly assert that nothing could be further from the truth—settles nothing. Whether the preferences we act on are evil is not something to be established by asking how strenuously we deny that they are; their moral status depends on whether by acting on them we are party to or complicit in the violation of someone's rights.

Are all those who act on evil preferences evil people? Not at all. As we noted in our earlier discussion of evil, people are evil (at least this is the clearest example of what we mean) when their general character leads them habitually to violate others' rights *and* to do so cruelly, either by taking pleasure in, or by being indifferent to, the suffering or loss caused by the violation. While some who benefit from animal rights' violations may meet this description, the majority of people, including those who, as part of their day-to-day lives, are supportive or tolerant of this evil, are not. In the vast majority of cases, I believe, people who support the meat industry by acting on their gustatory preferences are not evil people. And the same is true of the vast majority of those whose acquisitions support other animal abusing industries: they are not evil people either.

The judgment that otherwise decent people act on evil preferences in these ways may invite anger and resentment from some, hoots of derisive laughter from others; but it may also awaken still others to a larger sense of the moral significance of our lives, including (even) the moral significance of our most mundane choices: what we put in our mouths and wear on our backs. Imperfect creatures that we are, living in an imperfect world, not one of us can be entirely free from our role in the evil around us. That recognition of the rights of animals reveals far more evil than was previously suspected is no reason to deny the magnitude of the evil that exists in the world at large or how much we find in our own lives; rather, our common moral task is to search conscientiously for ways to lessen both.

RECONCILING INCONSISTENCIES

How has it come to pass that many of us, even as we genuinely care about animals, find ourselves supporting practices that are evil not only in their result but also in their origin? This is a question to give the most ardent animal rights advocate pause. Certainly I do not have a simple answer ready to hand. In fact, recent work by sociologists studying human attitudes and behavior suggests that animal rights is not an idea whose time has come.

In their studies of diverse human populations, Arnold Arluke and Clinton R. Sanders cite many of the "conflicts" and "contradictions" that characterize human–animal interactions. Do these conflicts and contradictions bother people? Hardly ever, according to the authors. Write Arluke and Sanders: "While inconsistency does occasionally come into an individual's awareness as a glaring problem calling for correction, most of the time, most people live comfortably with contradictions as a natural and normal part of everyday life." And, again: "[Living with contradictions] is not troublesome for ordinary persons because commonsense is not constrained to be consistent." For the great mass of humanity, then, loving animals and eating them, respecting animals and wearing them, are not matters to lose any sleep over.

History suggests that humans are made of sturdier stuff. If most of us, most of the time, really had no trouble living with contradictions, slavery would still be with us and women would still be campaigning for the vote. While some people some of the time may be able to live with some contradictions, some inconsistencies, there must be thresholds above which the daily business of living is affected. I clearly remember when this happened in my life. My reading of Gandhi awakened me to the realization that I held inconsistent beliefs and attitudes about unnecessary violence to human beings, on the one hand, and unnecessary violence to animal beings, on the other. And the death of a canine friend led me to the realization that I was placing some animals (dogs and cats, in particular) in one emotional category and other animals (hogs and calves, for example) in another, even as I realized that, when viewed in terms of their individual capabilities, there really was no relevant difference between them. Could I have "lived comfortably" with these contradictions? I don't think so. One way or another, I had to change.

I have no reason to believe my wanting to craft a coherent set of values for my life makes me any different from anyone else. None of us is so acculturated that we sleepwalk through our moral lives. If too few of us today are seriously troubled by our contradictory beliefs and attitudes toward animals, I believe this is because too few of us recognize where and why our beliefs and attitudes are contradictory. In particular, too few of us really know what is happening to animals, just as too few of us have ever paused to think carefully about their moral status. What is invisible, both in fact and in value, must first be made visible before it can be seen and understood; contradictions must first be honestly acknowledged before they can be honestly addressed. One of this volume's central purposes has been to use moral philosophy to help make some things more visible than before.

CHANGE

For reasons already adduced, the rights view supports the "radical," "extreme" views mentioned at the outset. It calls for the abolition of those industries that systematically violate the rights of animals, the meat and the fur industries, for example. To bring about change of this magnitude, sweeping in its aspirations, obviously is beyond the reach of any one person. Change of this kind (social change) can only happen over time as a result of the determined work of a critical mass of people, working collaboratively and imaginatively. I will have more to say about social change below.

The rights view also calls for change that is within the reach of each person. In particular, it calls on each of us to strive to make the world better by withholding our direct support from the major animal exploiting industries. This means we must strive to stop eating the flesh of animals, strive to stop wearing their pelts or skin, and strive to stop others from exploiting them in other ways (for example, using them as tools in their research). How we do this is a personal question that no moral theory can answer. Whether we should do this, when the question is asked as a moral question, finds an answer in moral theory.

This invitation to strive to live in ways that respect animal rights needs to be tempered with a heavy dose of realism. As long as we are alive in this world, we will be implicated in its evil, including the harmful things done to animals. Consider cotton clothes, for example. No animal fur or skin here. But cotton is one of the most chemically intensively raised crops in the world. Herbicides. Nematicides. Fungicides. All manner of chemical cides (*cide* means *death*) are administered to cotton. When the rains come (as they will) and the cides are washed into neighboring rivers and streams (as they will be), fish and other animals are killed. Before that, many land animals are killed when mechanized tillers prepare the earth for planting. The result? Anytime we buy something made from cotton, we take home clothes stained with the blood of animals.

The same is true in other areas of our lives. Vegetarians and vegans do not eat animal flesh, so no animal is intentionally or deliberately killed for their food. But countless numbers of animals are killed when fields are cleared or plowed to grow everything from avocados to zucchini. More, we all live in homes or apartments and travel on roadways that cover land formerly occupied by animals, now displaced, incalculably many of them injured or killed during the transition. Until we breathe our final breath, there is no way for us to escape being implicated in the evil animals suffer. Animals are going to be harmed no matter what we do, in part because of what we do. So why worry about eating meat or wearing fur?

Here is how I picture our shared situation. Imagine a large, intricate spider's web. The web has a center; it also has outer edges. Picture the web as representing the evil in the world. The worst things are at the center of the web; the least bad things are at the edges.

Where do we find the evil visited upon animals by the major animal user industries (animal agriculture, for example)? Here is what we have to take into account before we answer. The bodies of literally billions of animals are intentionally, deliberately, and systematically injured every year, year after year. The freedom of millions of animals is intentionally, deliberately, and systematically denied every minute of every day. The very lives of millions of animals is intentionally, deliberately, and systematically taken every hour of every day. People like me, who believe in animal rights, believe that what is being done to animals is at or near the center; it is this bad, in our view.

Where, then, do we find the evil visited upon animals by the cotton industry, for example? Not in the same neighborhood. The harm caused to animals by the cotton industry is not intentional, not deliberate, and not systematic. The same is true of the harm done when everything from avocados to zucchini is farmed. This makes a difference, when viewed from the perspective of the rights view. Our first duty is to remove our direct support from the major animal user industries by refusing to buy their products. We do not fail in this duty when we purchase other products, manufactured by other industries, though even here an expansive animal consciousness would counsel making do with less rather than making do with more. As is well and truly said, we should live simply so that others may simply live.

THE GROUNDS OF HOPE

Evidence suggests that more and more people are beginning to come to terms with the inconsistencies I have noted and are changing their lives as a result. At least in some cases, a critical mass is in the process of forming and social change is occurring. Take the fur industry, for example. As recently as the mid-1980s, seventeen million animals were trapped for their fur in the United States; by the early 1990s, that number was approximately ten million; today the number stands at four and one-half million.

During this same period the number of caged-mink "ranches" declined from one thousand to slightly over three hundred. In 1988, active trappers numbered 330,000; by 1994 there were fewer than half that number; today, approximately a third. Arizona, California, Colorado, Florida, Massachusetts, New Jersey, and Rhode Island have joined eighty-nine nations, from Austria to Zimbabwe, in banning use of the steel-jawed leghold trap. Internationally, Austria, England, Scotland, and Wales have passed legislation that prohibits raising mink and other animals solely or primarily for their fur, and Denmark and Norway have declared that fur mills are "ethically unacceptable." In the U.S. House of Representatives, legislation that would ban the use of the steel-jawed leghold trap on all federal lands garnered eighty-nine cosponsors from both major political parties. All the indicators point to the fur industry's steady downward spiral. Fur, once as "in" as anything could be in the world of fashion, increasingly is "out."

American consumption of most varieties of meat also is declining. Whereas fourteen million veal calves were slaughtered in 1945, the number stands at eight hundred thousand today. Except for poultry and fish, overall per capita meat consumption continues to decline. This same period has witnessed a decline in per capita consumption of eggs and dairy products. Granted, some people who have stopped eating meat and meat products, or who have decreased the amount that they eat, have done so for reasons other than respect for animal rights. Legitimate health and environmental concerns, for example, can lead some people to make changes in their diet. Nevertheless, the national trend away from an animal-based diet and toward one richer in vegetables, legumes, grains, and nuts is unmistakable.

Is reliance on the animal model in research, testing, and education undergoing a comparable transformation? Because exact numbers are hard to come by, no one can say with certainty. What is known is that there is a growing willingness on the part of the research community to look for ways of replacing animals in the lab, accelerated success in finding them, and a steady increase in the number of people who want to see this happen. Taking the lead among the governments of the world, the European Union in 2003 passed legislation that will prohibit cosmetics tests on animals, including the LD_{50}, in member nations by 2009; moreover, this same legislation bans the sale in the European Union of cosmetics that have been tested on animals anywhere. True, these bold moves do not stop all animal model research. Nevertheless, these are meaningful steps in the right direction, heralding the day when comparable legislation will become the law in America. The American public would seem to be ready. Recent polls conducted by the Associated Press and the Los Angeles Times found that 72 percent of those responding said that it is sometimes wrong to use animals in research, and fully 29 percent said it is always wrong.

Even the American public's attitude toward the idea of animal rights is changing. Once the object of ridicule and sarcasm, animal rights is increasingly accepted as an appropriate moral norm. According to the poll just alluded to, fully two-thirds of adult Americans agree that "an animal's right to live free from suffering should be just as important as a person's."

Is it, then, hopelessly unrealistic to imagine a day when fur coats will follow whalebone corsets into fashion oblivion, when slaughterhouses will exist only in history books, and when all the scientific laboratories of the world will have a sign over their entrances proclaiming No Animals Allowed? Those who are pessimistic about the moral possibilities of humanity will answer yes. And perhaps they are right. But those who believe in the human capacity to embrace both justice and compassion, not among isolated individuals but throughout the extended human family, will answer no. Not in my lifetime, perhaps, but someday surely, I believe, the principled journey to abolition, at the level of society, will be complete. As the evidence presented in the previous paragraphs suggests, in a variety of ways this long journey already has begun.

Social change to one side, many are the personal challenges we face, not only in the case of animal rights but in other important areas of our moral lives. How and why do people change their way of being in the world? I know enough to know that I do not know anything like the complete answer to this question. I do know one thing, however: some people have changed the direction of their lives in part because of what they learned by doing moral philosophy. All I need to do to confirm this is look in the mirror; I would not be the animal rights advocate I am today if I had not studied moral philosophy in the past. Let me conclude, therefore, by expressing the hope that this short introduction to the discipline will help motivate other people, in whatever modest ways it can, to make animal rights part of their lives. In such ways are the seeds of social change sometimes planted, one person at a time.

NOTES

Citations are arranged by subsections within each chapter.

CHAPTER 1 FROM INDIFFERENCE TO ADVOCACY

First Steps

I refer to Gandhi's autobiography, which changed the course of my life; I encourage everyone to read it. *An Autobiography: The Story of My Experiments with Truth* (Boston: Beacon Press, 1957).

My early essay on vegetarianism is "The Moral Basis of Vegetarianism," *The Canadian Journal of Philosophy* 5, no. 2 (October 1975): 181–214; reprinted in *All That Dwell Therein: Essays on Animal Rights and Environmental Ethics* (Berkeley: University of California Press, 1982), 1–39.

A Larger Consistency

Tolstoy wrote "The First Step" as the introduction to the Russian edition of Howard Williams's *The Ethics of Diet*, published in 1892. Excerpts from "The First Step" are included in Kerry S. Walters and Lisa Portness, eds., *Ethical Vegetarianism: From Pythagoras to Peter Singer* (Albany: State University of New York Press, 1999), 97–105.

"Animal Experimentation: First Thoughts," the essay in which I called for "a vast reduction in research involving animals," will also be found in *All That Dwell Therein*, 65–74. For a more thorough examination of all the issues discussed, both in those essays and in these pages, see my *The Case for Animal Rights* (Berkeley: University of California Press, 1983).

Looking Ahead

Thomas Taylor's *A Vindication of the Rights of Brutes* was originally published in 1792. It is available in a facsimile edition (Gainesville, Fla.: Scholars' Facsimiles & Reprints, 1966).

Father Rickaby's views are summarized in Tom Regan and Peter Singer, eds., *Animal Rights and Human Obligations* (Englewood Cliffs, N.J.: Prentice Hall, 1976), 180–81.

CHAPTER 2 ANIMAL EXPLOITATION

I discuss how the major animal industries exploit animals at greater length in *Empty Cages: Facing the Challenge of Animal Rights* (New York: Rowman & Littlefield, 2004). Additional information will be found at www.tomregan-animalrights.com.

Animals As Food

The estimate of eight hundred thousand milk-fed veal calves is given by the American Meat Institute at meatami.com/. Other numerical estimates are those of the U.S. Department of Agriculture at www.usda.gov/nass/pubs/histdata.htm.

Singer has revised and expanded *Animal Liberation*, 2nd ed. (New York: New York Review of Books, 1990). His references to *The Stall Street Journal* appear in chapter 3, "Down on the Factory Farm."

Repetitive motion and other behavioral signs of maladjustment of animals in intensive rearing systems were first documented in Britain by an independent government-appointed committee, headed by zoologist Professor F. W. Rogers Brambell. See *Report of the Technical Committee to Enquire into the Welfare of Animals Kept under Intensive Livestock Husbandry Systems* (London: Her Majesty's Stationary Office, 1965). A second study, *Animal Welfare in Poultry, Pig and Veal Calf Production* (London: Her Majesty's Stationary Office, 1981), submitted by the House of Commons' Agriculture Committee, was highly critical of the intensive rearing methods that continue to dominate contemporary American animal agribusiness. A brief overview of scientific studies of animal welfare is Joy A. Mench, "Thirty Years after Brambell: Whither Animal Welfare Science," *Journal of Applied Animal Welfare Science* 1, no. 2: 91–102. A more detailed account covering the same period is Richard Ryder, *The Political Animal: The Conquest of Speciesism* (Jefferson, N.C.: McFarland and Company, 1998); see, in particular, chapter 3, "The Science of Animal Welfare." Ryder coined the word *speciesism*.

Factory Farming

General surveys of factory farming include Michael W. Fox, *Farm Animals: Husbandry, Behavior, and Veterinary Practice* (Baltimore: University Park Press, 1984), and Jim Mason and Peter Singer, *Animal Factories* (New York: Crown, 1980).

Animals As Clothes

For the USDA's position on vegetarianism and veganism, see the fourth edition of *Dietary Guidelines for Americans* (Washington, D.C.: Government Printing Office, 1995). Also available at www.nalusda.gov/fnic/dga/dga95/cover.html.

Fur Mill Fur

Statistics concerning fur production come from the Fur Industry of America and can be confirmed at www.fur.org/furfarm.html.

Trapping

The estimate of the number of trappers I owe to Merritt Clifton, who bases this figure on two state-by-state censuses, one conducted by the Animal Welfare Institute, the other by the Humane Society of the United States.

The quotation of Desmond Morris appears in Mark Glover, "Eye of the Beholder," *The Animals' Voice Magazine* 5, no. 4 (1992): 33. Morris also addresses trapping in *The Animal Contract: An Impassioned and Rational Guide to Sharing the Planet and Saving Our Common World* (New York: Warner, 1990): 116–18. My thanks to Laura Moretti for locating these sources.

Friends of Animals literature on fur can be obtained on request from Friends of Animals, 777 Post Road, Darien, CT 06820, or at www.friendsof animals.org.

Animals As Tools

The Physicians Committee for Responsible Medicine, the Association of Veterinarians for Animal Rights, and the Medical Research Modernization Committee are among the groups of medically trained professionals who oppose using animals in research.

The statistics concerning the toxicity of FDA-approved drugs will be found in U.S. General Accounting Office, *Report to the Chairman, Subcommittee on Human Resources and Intergovernmental Relations, Committee on Government Operations, House of Representatives, FDA Drug Review, Postapproval Risk, 1976–1985* (Washington, D.C.: U.S. Government Printing Office, 1990).

The estimate of 1 percent of adverse drug reactions that are reported is given in D. A. Kessler, "Introducing MedWatch: A New Approach to Reporting Medication and Adverse Effects and Product Problems," *Journal of the American Medical Association* 269 (1993): 2765–68.

The estimate of 60 percent of total health costs attributable to smoking is included in a comprehensive economic analysis prepared by Robert Shubinski, M.D. and available at unr.edu/homepage/shubink/smokost1.html#cost2.

For an overview of how much the benefits of animal research are exaggerated and the harms understated, see Hugh LaFollette and Niall Shanks, *Brute Science: Dilemmas of Animal Experimentation* (New York: Rowman & Littlefield, 1996). In addition, see C. Ray Greek, MD and Jean Swingle Greek, DVM, *Sacred Cows and Golden Geese: The Human Costs of Experiments on Animals* (New York: Continuum, 2000), and *Specious Science: How Genetics and Evolution Reveal Why Medical Research on Animals Harms Humans* (New York: Continuum, 2002).

The LD$_{50}$

For a classic discussion of the variability in LD$_{50}$ results because of environmental and other factors, see R. Loosli, "Duplicate Testing and Reproducibility," in Regamay, Hennesen, Ikic, and Ungar, *International Symposium on Laboratory Medicine* (Basel: S. Krarger, 1967).

The passage by Ryder is from his *Victims of Science: The Use of Animals in Research* (London: Davis-Poyter, 1975), 36.

CHAPTER 3 THE NATURE AND IMPORTANCE OF RIGHTS

Different philosophers understand rights differently. I understand rights as valid claims. What this means is explained in chapter 6. In my judgment, the most powerful defense of viewing rights in this way will be found in the work of Joel Feinberg, including his classic essay "The Nature and Value of Rights," *The Journal of Value Inquiry* 4 (Winter 1970): 243–57.

Three excellent online bibliographies on human rights are "A Bibliography of Readings on Rights," compiled by William A. Edmundson at law.gsu.edu/wedmundson/Syllabi/rightbib.htm; "Hippias: Limited Area Search of Philosophy on the Internet" at hippias.evansville.edu/search.cgi?human + rights; and "A Bibliographical Survey of Philosophical Literature on Human Rights" at ethics.acusd.edu/theories/rights/.

Moral Integrity: No Trespassing

The idea that negative moral rights are like invisible No Trespassing signs I owe to Robert Nozick. See his *Anarchy, State, and Utopia* (New York: Basic Books, 1974).

Moral Weight: Trump

The status of rights as trump I owe to Ronald Dworkin, *Taking Rights Seriously* (London: Duckworth, 1977).

Animal Rights?

Carl Cohen's statement concerning why animal experimentation is wrong, if animals have rights, is from "Do Animals Have Rights?" *Ethics and Behavior* 7, no. 2 (1997): 92. Cohen's arguments against animal rights are reviewed in chapter 8.

CHAPTER 4 INDIRECT DUTY VIEWS

Polling results concerning both meat consumption and attitudes toward using animals to test medical treatments are among those found in a December 2, 1995 Associated Press telephone poll of 1,004 randomly selected adult Americans. The percentages concerning wearing fur come from a December 27, 1993, nationwide poll of 1,612 adults conducted by the Los Angeles Times. Exaggerated claims sometimes have been made regarding the number of vegetarians in the United States. In 2000 the Vegetarian Resource Group commissioned a Zogby poll. Respondents (968 women and men over age eighteen) were interviewed by telephone. The result: approximately 2.5 percent, or 4.8

million, of the estimated 193 million Americans over eighteen, excluding those who are institutionalized, "never eat red meat, never eat poultry, never eat fish."

Results of the Zogby poll are available at www.vgr.org. For a discussion of the other polls, see Harold Herzog, Andrew Rowan, and Daniel Kossow, "Social Attitudes and Animals," *The State of Animals, 2001*, available at files .hsus.org/web-files/PDF/MARK_State_of_Animals_Ch_03.pdf.

Cartesianism Then and Now

Descartes's views about animals may be found in selections from his work in Tom Regan and Peter Singer, eds., *Animal Rights and Human Obligations*, 13–20.

The quotation of Nicholas Fontaine appears in Lenora Rosenfield, *From Beast-Machine to Man-Machine* (New York: Columbia, 1968), 54.

For the views of Peter Carruthers, see *The Animals Issue: Moral Theory in Practice* (Cambridge: Cambridge University Press, 1992), especially chapter 8. Carruthers allows for the possibility that extraterrestrials might be conscious despite the fact that they do not use a natural language; among terrestrials, however, the ability to use such a language is necessary for conscious experience. Another neo-Cartesian, Peter Harrison, offers a quite different argument for why animals do not feel pain in "Theodicy and Animal Pain," *Philosophy* 64 (January 1989): 79–92. The views of both Carruthers and Harrison are critically examined by Evelyn Pluhar in the first chapter of *Beyond Prejudice: The Moral Significance of Human and Nonhuman Animals* (Durham: Duke University Press, 1995). Pluhar's book includes an excellent bibliography.

Science and Animal Minds

Voltaire's response to Descartes may be found in *Animal Rights and Human Obligations*, 20.

Darwin's views are summarized in *Animal Rights and Human Obligations*, 27–31. This anthology also includes several other important contributions to the literature on animal minds. For a contemporary elaboration and defense of Darwin's approach and conclusions, along with an excellent bibliography, see Colin Allen and Marc Bekoff, *Species of Mind: The Philosophy and Biology of Cognitive Ethology* (Cambridge: MIT Press, c1997).

Bird cognition studies are summarized by Monica Amarelo, " 'Bird Brains' Take Heart: Our Feathered Friends Are No Slouch at Cognition," American

Association for the Advancement of Science, February 14, 2002; available at www.eurekalert.org/pub_releases/2002–02/aaft-bt020602.php.

For information about scrub jay cognition, see Susan Milius, "Birds with a Criminal Past Hide Food Well," *Science News Online*, November 6, 2002. Available at www.phschool.com/science/science_news/articles/bird_criminal _past.html.

Thelma Lee Gross, DVM, DACVP, "Scientific and Moral Consideration for Live Animal Practice," *Journal of the American Veterinary Medical Association* 222, No. 3 (February 1, 2003), 285–88.

The summary of fish cognition is taken from Redouan Bishary, Wolfgang Wickler, and Hans Fricke, "Fish Cognition: A Primate's Eye View," *Animal Cognition* 5 (2002), 1–13. The authors present their findings as "purely functional."

Simple Contractarianism

The simple form of contractarianism I sketch takes its inspiration from some of Jan Narveson's earlier writings. See his "Animal Rights," *Canadian Journal of Philosophy* 2 (March 1977): 161–78, and "Animal Rights Revisited," in H. Miller and W. Williams, eds., *Ethics and Animals* (Clifton, N.J.: Humana Press, 1983), 56–58.

Rawlsian Contractarianism

John Rawls's *A Theory of Justice* was first published by Harvard University Press in 1971. It is possible to interpret his position either narrowly or broadly. The narrow interpretation assumes that what Rawls argues is restricted to justice only; the broad interpretation assumes that what he argues is not restricted to justice only but is, instead, offered as a general account of moral right and wrong. I favor the latter interpretation and believe that the criticisms I suggest, if modified appropriately, could be pressed equally forcefully against the narrow interpretation. Rawls's description of the original position will be found on p. 130; his characterization of a "sense of justice" on p. 505; the requirement that those covered by whatever principles are adopted must be able "to understand and act upon (them)" on p. 137; and the extension of the procedures he favors to include "the choice of all ethical principles" on p. 130.

A Theory of Justice has occasioned a voluminous literature. Important relevant discussions are Mark Rowlands, "Contractarianism and Animals," *Jour-*

nal of Applied Philosophy 14, no. 3 (1997): 235–47; Mark H. Bernstein, *On Moral Considerability: An Essay on Who Matters Morally* (Oxford: Oxford University Press, 1998), 151–58; and Peter Carruthers, *The Animals Issue*, 101–3.

Evaluating Rawlsian Contractarianism

Issac Parker's testimony before Great Britain's House of Commons Select Committee is quoted in Roger Antsey, *The Atlantic Slave Trade and British Abolition: 1760–1810* (Atlantic Highlands, N.J.: Humanities Press, 1975), 32.

Speciesism

Carl Cohen defends speciesism in his contribution to our jointly authored book, *The Animal Rights Debate* (New York: Rowman & Littlefield, 2002), 59–65.

CHAPTER 5 DIRECT DUTY VIEWS

The Cruelty-Kindness View

The quotations of Kant may be found in Regan and Singer, *Animal Rights and Human Obligations*, 24.

The quotation of Locke appears in James Axtfell, ed., *The Educational Writings of John Locke* (Cambridge: Cambridge University Press, 1968), 225–26.

Social scientists have demonstrated a pattern of childhood abuse of animals among convicted violent criminals. See, for example, Stephen R. Keller and Alan R. Felthouse, "Childhood Cruelty toward Animals among Criminals and Non Criminals," *Human Relations* 38 (1985): 1113–29. For a more recent work devoted to the same subject, see Randall Lockwood and Frank R. Ascione, eds., *Cruelty to Animals and Interpersonal Violence: Readings in Research and Application* (West Lafayette, Ind.: Purdue University Press, 1998).

Evaluating Cruelty-Kindness

The quotation from Joan Dunayer is from her *Animal Equality: Language and Liberation* (Derwood, Md.: Ryce Publishing, 2001), 107.

The interview with Donny Tice and Alec Wainwright from which I quote will be found in Gail Eisnitz, *Slaughterhouse: The Shocking Greed, Neglect, and Inhumane Treatment inside the U.S. Meat Industry* (Amherst, N.Y.: Prometheus Books, 1997), 97–98.

Utilitarianism

For Peter Singer's views regarding ethics and animals, see *Animal Liberation*, and *Practical Ethics* (Cambridge: Cambridge University Press, 1979). Singer's views regarding irreplaceability and the wrongness of killing are more fully developed in the latter work than they are in the former.

Among R. G. Frey's relevant publications are *Interests and Rights: The Case against Animals* (Oxford: Clarendon Press, 1980) and *Rights, Killing, and Suffering* (Oxford: Basil Blackwell, 1983).

Evaluating Preference Utilitarianism

For a detailed examination of the rape case, see Bernard Lefkowitz, *Our Guys: The Glen Ridge Rape and the Secret Life of the Perfect Suburb* (Berkeley: University of California Press, 1997).

A possible account of evil preferences would include preferences other than those that are tied to rights violations. People who gratuitously deface or destroy works of art, for example, might be construed to be acting on evil preferences even if works of art lack rights. For present purposes, this matter can be left unresolved. It is enough that my account offers a sufficient condition for classifying preferences as evil.

Singer's online defense of bestiality will be found in his review of Midas Dekker's *Dearest Pet: On Bestiality* at www.nerve.com/Opinions/Singer/heavyPetting/.

Statistical Abstract of the United States is available online at www.census .gov/prod/www/statistical-abstract-us.html.

CHAPTER 6 HUMAN RIGHTS

Kant's most relevant work is *The Fundamental Principles of the Metaphysic of Morals*, available in many editions. Kant himself would not extend rights to nonhuman animals. For a statement of his indirect duty view, see the selection from his writings in *Animal Rights and Human Obligations*, 23–24.

Moral Elitism

Excerpts from Aristotle's work, where his commitment to moral elitism is starkly evident, are included in *Animal Rights and Human Obligations*, 53–56.

Persons

See Kant, *The Fundamental Principles*.
For further discussion of the overemphasis of persons in moral philosophy, see my "Putting People in Their Place," *Defending Animal Rights* (Urbana: University of Illinois Press, 2001), 86–105.

The Children of Willowbrook

A useful account of the research conducted on the children of Willowbrook is David J. Rothman and Shelia Rothman, *The Willowbrook Wars* (New York: Harper & Row, 1984). The description of the symptoms of Hepatitis B is given on p. 268.

Subjects-of-a-Life

For Bill Lawson's discussion of lexical gaps, see "Moral Discourse and Slavery," Howard McGary and Bill Lawson, eds., *Between Slavery and Freedom: Philosophy and American Slavery* (Bloomington: Indiana University Press, 1992), 71–89.

For an exhaustive review of recent work on fetal and neonatal brain development, which includes an extensive bibliography, see Charles D. Laughlin, "Pre- and Perinatal Brain Development and Enculturation: A Biogenetic Structural Approach," available on the web at superior.carleton.ca/~claughli/dn-art1a.htm. Writes Laughlin:

> The literature in pre- and perinatal psychology (including aspects of cognitive psychology, developmental psychology, developmental neuropsychology, psychobiology, social psychobiology and clinical psychology) now provides ample evidence that the perceptual and cognitive competence of the fetus and infant is significantly greater than was once thought. This evidence suggests that neurocognitive development in the pre- and perinatal human being produces structures that make the world of experience "already there" for the advanced fetus, neonate and infant. For instance, objects, relations between objects, faces and speech sounds appear to be already meaningful to the neonate.

Objections to the Rights View

R. G. Frey's criticism will be found in "Autonomy and the Value of Life," *Monist* 7, no. 1 (1987): 58.

Peter Singer, "Utilitarianism and Vegetarianism," *Philosophy and Public Affairs* 9, no. 8 (Summer 1980): 326. Singer argues this point at greater length in his "Sidgwick and Reflective Equilibrium," *The Monist* 58, no. 3 (July 1974): especially 515–17.

Dan Brock, "Utilitarianism," in Tom Regan and Donald VanDeVeer, eds., *And Justice for All* (Towata, N.J.: Rowman & Littlefield, 1981), 223.

For a fuller discussion and defense of appeals to intuition, see my *The Case for Animal Rights*, chapter 4.

A number of philosophers have objected to the rights view by arguing for the extension of inherent value to nonsentient nature. Of particular note are Holmes Rolston, III, *Environmental Ethics: Duties to and Values in the Natural World* (Philadelphia: Temple University Press, 1988); J. Baird Callicott, "Non-Anthropocentric Value Theory and Environmental Ethics," *American Philosophical Quarterly* 21 (1984): 299–309; and Paul Taylor, *Respect for Nature* (Princeton: Princeton University Press, 1986). For my critical reservations about the possible success of this enterprise, see "Does Environmental Ethics Rest on a Mistake?" *The Monist* 75 (1992): 161–82.

CHAPTER 7 ANIMAL RIGHTS

A more thorough argument for animal rights will be found in *The Case for Animal Rights*. This work also addresses how to resolve conflicts in rights, a topic not discussed in these pages.

Two excellent online bibliographies on animal rights are "The Moral Status of Animals," compiled by Lawrence M. Hinman at ethics.acusd.edu/Applied/animals/, and "Hippias: Limited Area Search of Philosophy on the Internet" at hippias.evansville.edu/search.cgi?animal+rights.

CHAPTER 8 OBJECTIONS AND REPLIES

Religious Objections

"Animals Do Not Have Souls."

Whether animals have souls is a much debated question; some well-regarded theologians answer in the affirmative. For a sampling of the relevant literature, including John Wesley's views, see Tom Regan and Andrew Linzey, eds., *Animals and Christianity: A Book of Readings* (New York: Crossroad, 1989).

Philosophical Objections

For additional responses to philosophical critics of my position, see "The Case for Animal Rights: A Decade's Passing," Richard T. Hull, ed., *A Quarter Century of Value Inquiry: Presidential Addresses of the American Society for Value Inquiry* (Amsterdam: Rodopi, 1994), 439–59. This essay can also be found in *Defending Animal Rights*, 39–65.

Cohen's First Objection

The quotation about the lioness and the baby zebra occurs in Carl Cohen, *The Animal Rights Debate*, 30–31.

Cohen's Second Objection

Cohen's "right kind" argument is offered in *The Animal Rights Debate*, 37.

Cohen's Third Objection

Cohen's "community" argument is offered in "Do Animals Have Rights?" *Ethics and Behavior* 7, no. 2: 94–95.

My response to Cohen's objections is adapted from my discussion of his views in Carl Cohen and Tom Regan, *The Animal Rights Debate*, 271–84.

CHAPTER 9 MORAL PHILOSOPHY AND CHANGE

Reconciling Inconsistencies

The quotations of Arluke and Sanders are from their *Regarding Animals* (Philadelphia: Temple University Press, 1996), 190 and 188, respectively.

THE GROUNDS OF HOPE

Information about annual meat consumption in the United States is based on "Food Consumption Overview," provided by the Economic Research Service, U.S. Department of Agriculture; available at www.ers.usda.gov/briefing/ consumption/overview.htm.

Information about the European Union's change in cosmetic testing can be found at the British Union for the Abolition of Vivisection's website: www .buav.org/f_campaign.html.

The Los Angeles Times and other public opinion polls are discussed in Harold Herzog, Andrew Rowan, and Daniel Kossow, "Social Attitudes and Animals," *The State of Animals, 2001,* available at files.hsus.org/web-files/ PDF/MARK_State_of_Animals_Ch_03.pdf.

INDEX

animal awareness, reasons for believing in: commonsense, 35, 38; evolution, 35–39; religious teachings, 38–39
animal rights: importance of the issue, xii, xiii, 29–30; general objections and replies to, 99–104; and personal change, 121; philosophical objections and replies to, 108–13; and practical questions, 96–98; public's changing attitude toward, 121; and questions of fact, 91–92; and questions of logic, 94–96; and questions of value, 92–94; religious objections and replies to, 104–7; ridiculed, 7; and social change, 118, 119–21; summary of cumulative argument for, 95–96
animal rights advocates: characterizations of, xi
animal rights movement, 1, 96
animal use: in agriculture, 9–13, 97; in fashion, 13–17; in science, 17–20, 97, 120
Animal Welfare Act, 20
appeals to intuition, 85–86, 133
Aristotle, 72, 132
Arluke, Arnold, 117

bestiality: the right's view's position on, 98; Singer's approval of, 63, 131

birds, 37, 128, 129
Blumberg, Baruch, 79
Brock, Dan, 85, 133

Carruthers, Peter, 34–35, 39, 50, 95, 128
Cartesians, 34, 35, 39, 49, 50, 94. See Descartes
children of Willowbrook, 82
Cohen, Carl, 28, 29, 30, 48–49, 111–13, 127, 130, 134
contractarianism. See Rawlsian contractarianism; simple contractarianism
cruelty, 51, 53–55; indifferent, 53, 55; sadistic, 53, 55. See also evil
cruelty-kindness view: evaluated, 54–57; and evil, 88; explained, 51–54; moral standing in, 53–54; and prejudice, 52; strengths, 53–53

Darwin, Charles, 35–36, 37, 128
Descartes, Rene, 34–36, 128
direct duties, 27; to animals, 49–50, 95
direct duty views, 51–66
Dunayer, Joan, 54, 130
duty of respect, 68, 69–71, 73, 78, 79, 83; Kant and, 78, 79

ABOUT THE AUTHOR

Tom Regan (Emeritus Professor of Philosophy, North Carolina State University) is universally recognized as the intellectual leader of the animal rights movement. During his more than thirty years on the faculty, he received numerous awards for excellence in undergraduate and graduate teaching; was named University Alumni Distinguished Professor; published hundreds of professional papers and more than twenty books; won major international awards for film writing and direction; and presented hundreds of lectures throughout the United States and abroad. Upon his retirement in 2001, he received the William Quarles Holliday Medal, the highest honor N.C. State University can bestow on one of its faculty. In that same year, using his donated papers and his extensive personal library as the foundation, the North Carolina State University Library established the Tom Regan Animal Rights Archive. Enriched by the addition of newly donated materials, the collection is the world's leading archival resource for animal rights scholarship. Information about Tom Regan's career and the archive named in his honor is available at http://www.lib.ncsu.edu/arights/

He is married to the former Nancy Tirk, with whom he co-founded The Culture & Animals Foundation <cultureandanimals.org>.